# • • • contents • • •

T0204808

ello, dear reader! We're going to be spending some time together, so I'd like to honor our relationship from the very beginning. I'm grateful that you've picked up this book and that you're willing to journey with me through these pages. I hope and pray that something in them will be helpful to you.

If you're anything like me, I'm guessing your life isn't perfectly put together, perfectly in sync with your values, perfectly satisfying and fulfilling. I imagine you may have some intuition, deep in your heart and your bones, that something is a little amiss—or perhaps a lot amiss—in your own life and in the wider life of our culture. Perhaps you're thinking, as I often do, that we've all been sold a bill of goods—that with all of the goodies and gadgets served up to us, we should feel happier, more fulfilled, and more peaceful than we actually do. Most of us have more conveniences and luxuries than any previous generation could have even imagined, and yet it may feel that there's something missing, something off, some sort of emptiness at the core of it—and that at the end of the day, we feel more the slave than the master of our stuff, our services, and our schedules.

I'm writing this book because I have felt all of those things and still feel them to a large degree. I have to think that these feelings of dis-ease are clues that another, more beautiful sort of life is possible, both for you and me and for our communities and culture at large. My hope at the beginning of the COVID-19 pandemic was that we would come out of it more equipped and motivated to pursue such a life, and here in the midst of it, that hope remains. I'd like to explore what sort of interior attitudes and exterior decisions would make for a life that felt more at ease, more satisfying, more connected with things that are real and important—a life that contributed to healthy communities and a healthy planet.

As I've wrestled with these questions over the years, and as I've talked with others who have done similar wrestling, a theme that keeps resurfacing is simplicity. Jesus was a simple carpenter; he called his disciples by asking them to leave everything and follow him, and he had plenty to say about those who were encumbered by their possessions and entangled in their commitments. The idea of simplicity runs throughout monasticism, from the early desert fathers and mothers through the established religious orders. It's been exemplified in the lives of saints, most famously in St. Francis, the humble beggar of Assisi. It's even been picked up in recent years by young hipsters, older hippies, and plenty of folks in between who want to be less encumbered by the trappings and demands of modern life. Many are saying no to various aspects of the American Dream, seeking instead to invest in relationships, community service, leisure activity, and alternatives to nine-to-five employment. Across these various contexts, the common denominator seems to be that simplicity is a key to an authentic, satisfying life.

I'd like to explore the idea of simplicity with you and see what role it can and should play in a well-lived life. Rough-and-ready, my working definition of simplicity is making intentional lifestyle choices that create the freedom we need to honor the deepest needs of ourselves, the wider concentric circles of human relationships, and God's gift of the natural world.

Before I unpack that definition and reflect on where it will take us in this book, let me give you a little background. I'm going to be sharing some personal stories and examples throughout this book, so at the beginning of the journey, I'd like to give you some context.

Once upon a time, I was a driven, ambitious young college student with the strange combination of an engineer's mind, a love of literature, and an abiding curiosity about all things spiritual and philosophical. In my first year of college, that drive and ambition collided with two people who would become mentors to me: the Kentucky farmer poet Wendell Berry and the Quaker conservationist writer Scott Russell Sanders. Through their published writing, through letters, and through personal relationships, these two helped me start asking important vocational questions about what makes for a well-lived life. They awakened me to a deep care for the natural world and for the health of human beings and human communities—we who have the daunting responsibility to keep this blue-green planet healthy and fruitful for our own and subsequent generations. Scott especially, but Wendell also in his poetic way, introduced me to the quiet power of the contemplative life as a way to discover the life of the Spirit running through creation and through my own soul—and as a practical way to stay sane and centered amidst the bumpy ride of early adulthood.

They ruined the me that had some pretty clear (and pretty grand) plans for my future. Scott helped upend my earnest and comfortable mainline Protestant faith, and he set me on spiritual path that would wind through various Christian denominations, a flirtation with Hinduism, a fascination with Buddhism that I've kept to this day, and the pursuit of a Master of Divinity. That winding path would finally, several years later, lead me to join the Roman Catholic Church, in love with its incarnational theology, its mystics and saints, and its deep ethical commitments to social justice and (more recently) to environmental stewardship. These two mentors also ruined much of my ambition. Or rather they transmogrified it into a desire to live a well-crafted life that aligned with my values, even if that life would likely look unconventional to most and wouldn't meet the standards of "success" that I absorbed from the go-go-go zeitgeist of the 1980s, when I came of age.

These mentors awakened me to a set of values that would provide a means to navigate the choices I faced as a young adult trying to find my way. They gave me a set of questions to ask of my life and my life choices, helping me to see those choices with more clarity and perspective. What sort of life will nurture my spiritual growth and open my heart to God? What sort of life will serve healthy relationships, from the family to the neighborhood and beyond to the city, the country, and the entire human family? What sort of life will help ensure that our planet will be beautiful, healthy, and fruitful for subsequent generations?

My time in graduate school was at once an immersion in the lofty world of theological study and, in my spare time and during some ministry placements, an immersion in the world of urban community gardening. Finally, a little more than a year after my graduation, I gave myself fully to the idealistic vision that had been simmering in me for years, threw caution and prudence to the wind, and bought a piece of rough land in my home state of Indiana, with the goal of making an organic farm out of it.

Thus commenced a fifteen-year experiment with simple living, which I've described more fully in a previous book, *A Time to Plant: Life Lessons in Work, Prayer, and Dirt.* It began in as simple, stripped-down a way as you can imagine: I lived (or rather, camped) for close to a year without electricity, indoor plumbing, heat, a refrigerator, or any conveniences whatsoever. By turns, I shivered, sweated, swatted mosquitoes, and shooed mice off my cot and sleeping bag. During this time, I built a barn, finished out part of it as a small bachelor-pad apartment, and wired it up with a small solar-power system. I had been putting the finishing touches on my super-simple hermit life when I met Cyndi, the woman who would become my wife and would change my life—not least by inspiring me to install an honest-to-goodness flushable toilet in order to woo her. Over the next few years, Cyndi and I welcomed three beautiful children to join us in our off-the-grid, back-to-the-land life. At one point four of us (we started out with identical twins) were stuffed into that made-for-one, bachelor-pad apartment while I worked doggedly to finish a green, super-efficient home we designed and built almost entirely ourselves. At the same time we were trying to hold a farm together, and I was working a full-time job to keep everything bankrolled. Those early years were strenuous and stressful; things felt impossibly busy, complicated, and compromised. At times I found myself yearning for the roughing-it simplicity of my bachelor days. Over the years on that farm, though, we gradually found a rhythm of work and rest that felt more sustainable, and we rejoiced in the marvelous, grace-filled challenge of tending our marriage, tending our farm, and raising our kids to say yes to the satisfying, simple pleasures of close-to-nature living.

Then we did the unimaginable: after a decade and a half of investing untold thousands of hours of love, blood, sweat, tears, and joy, we sold that farm and left that life. The reasons were brutally simple. Cyndi, who stayed at home with our children, felt isolated and lonely out on our rural homestead. I had been running graduate theology and ministry formation programs at Saint Meinrad, a Catholic seminary and school of theology around the corner from our farm, and I was beginning to feel restless and confined in that work. I yearned for new professional challenges that I could not find in our rural county. After a few years of struggling with this, I stumbled

upon a dream job opportunity in Louisville: running an interfaith spirituality center committed to meditation and contemplative practice, social justice, compassion, and care for the
Earth. Taking that job would mean leaving the farm in order
to move closer to Louisville, but after some hemming and
hawing, I applied. I was offered the position, and my family
and I discerned that God was calling me to this new work and
our family to a new life in a new place.

It's been over six years since we sold our farm to a dear
couple we knew from our old parish. I'm grateful that the farm
is in their good hands, but I'll admit that, even after several
years, I still struggle to let that place go. On the other hand,
the home we purchased closer to Louisville has eight acres
of rugged woods, so between gardening, cutting firewood to
heat our home, and other back-to-the-land sorts of activities,
I've been able to continue some of the same practices that
were so meaningful on the farm. And the work of running
the Earth & Spirit Center has been more satisfying (and more
challenging) than I ever could have hoped or dreamed; it's an
integration of the broadest cross-section of my values, interests, and skills. In a strange irony, so much of what I had
tried to do on the farm by myself would end up being done in
community on the twenty-seven-acre Earth & Spirit Center
campus. Over the years we've started a communal farm for
African refugees; planted a permaculture food forest; built
wetlands, pollinator gardens, and rain gardens; and tackled
a whole host of other environmental projects, all woven into
programming that prioritizes contemplative practice and
concern for social justice.

Even so, I continue to struggle with what simplicity means for me and my family in this new context. On the one hand, our home life is quite a bit *simpler* than it was on the farm. As I'll explore more in a later chapter, living a back-to-the-land life, especially on a farm, can actually be quite complicated and involved. On the other hand, my work life is busy and hectic, my commute is long (albeit in an electric car), and like most of us, I'm pulled in a lot of different directions personally and professionally. In fact, before undertaking this book project, I had to think long and hard about whether I had the time and energy to bring it over the finish line. Did you catch that wonderful irony? I was asking: Is my life too busy to write a book about simplicity? If I had to ask a question like that, did I have any right to write about simplicity for others?

I have my doubts, but I'll let you be the judge of that. What I *can* say is that I've been in various places on the spectrum in terms of commitment to and practice of the amorphous term *simplicity*. Along with my family, I'm still trying to figure out what kind of life is spiritually nurturing, socially just, and environmentally sustainable, given our gifts, commitments, and evolving circumstances. I'm beginning to realize that my answer to that question is a moving target rather than a single, static solution—and of course, my answer will be different in many ways from yours. But I hope that as I share some of my own journey and reflections, they will be helpful to you on your path, however similar to or different from mine it may be. There is no one mold here. There are only, I hope, common values, common basic human needs, and the common ground beneath our feet: this one, beautiful, God-given, wonderful, wounded planet that we all share.

Having said a few words about my story, I offer a few about style and substance. This book isn't a philosophical exhortation on the moral necessity of "living simply so that others may simply live," although we'll certainly explore issues of justice, fair share, and solidarity along the way—and we'll even reflect a bit on the idea of virtue. Neither is this book a sales pitch for simplicity and minimalism as lifestyle statements and tribal identity markers. Finally, this book isn't about simplicity as the way to avert social and ecological Armageddon. All of these—moral rectitude, social prestige, and catastrophizing—are external concerns of the ego, and while the ego has a rightful place in our thinking and our choices, it should be, at best, first mate rather than captain. The spiritual journey, on the other hand, as many saints and contemplatives have reminded us over the centuries, is an inward journey, one of lessening the ego's grip on us and instead making room for the still, soft voice of the divine to guide our hearts into greater harmony with God, with our own best self, with others, and with the glory of creation. I'm interested in exploring with you the twists and turns of that journey, discerning what kind of life choices make for true wholeness, happiness, and holiness. I believe—and I'll try to convince you—that if we make those kinds of choices, we'll not only have richer lives as individuals, but our communities will be stronger and God's creation will be healthier for it.

I've been deeply formed by my Christian faith, growing up in various Protestant denominations and having been in the Roman Catholic Church for two decades of my adult life. I've always had ecumenical instincts, believing that truths can be found in a variety of traditions. I've seen this proven out again and again in the last several years running an interfaith spirituality center that weaves together contemplative spiritual practices from various religious traditions. While most of the language and metaphors of this book are rooted in Christianity, I'm not going to be shy about including the wisdom from other traditions (including the secular mindfulness tradition), because these other voices have been tremendously helpful to me on my journey.

I should also confess that I have struggled—and do struggle—with my own doubts, both in terms of my own individual faith and especially in regard to the religious institutions that have formed me and to which I remain stubbornly loyal. I see my faith, and the institutional forms of Christianity, as constantly evolving in response to new experiences and knowledge. That's not to say there aren't solid, abiding truths in Christianity; I believe there are. But there's also plenty of gray in my own thinking and beliefs. For all its beauty, I think there is plenty of ambiguity in institutional Christianity as well. All this is to say that I hope you will find this book helpful (or at least not offensive) not only if you have strong commitments to the Christian faith, but also if you have become alienated from the Christian tradition or never had much grounding in it in the first place.

Finally, from story, style, and substance to structure. I've divided this book into two parts. In "Why Simplicity?" I put forward four main reasons I think it makes sense to embrace simplicity as a lifestyle commitment. The first is that in most cases, and by almost every meaningful measure, simplifying our lives tends to bring us more pleasure, happiness, satisfaction, and contentment. The second, for those of us who have strong inclinations or commitments to spiritual growth, simplicity offers an invitation to a deeper and richer spiritual life. I don't think it's a coincidence that many of the great spiritual leaders and saints—Jesus, St. Paul, St. Benedict, St. Francis, Gandhi, St. Teresa of Calcutta, and our current Pope Francis, to name only a few—have lived lives and preached messages that embody simplicity.

If the first two pillars of my case for simplicity are personal and interior—pleasure and spiritual growth—the other two are outward-facing and communal, recognizing that in a world as spiritually and materially interconnected as ours is revealing itself to be, the inward journey is inextricably woven into outward circumstances. So my third reason to consider simplicity as a cornerstone practice is one of solidarity with those whose lives are simple by necessity rather than choice. When I think of the poor, I certainly think of the "bottom billion" who face a heartbreaking struggle for the basic necessities of life, and several more billion who are just one illness, injury, dowry, or missed paycheck away from joining them. Most of us think that kind of poverty exists only across the globe in other nations we (often condescendingly) call the "third" or "developing" world, but there is plenty of grinding poverty in our own country—in American cities (especially in highly segregated cities like Louisville) and in struggling rural areas. I believe that if we are ever to have healthy local communities, nations, and a thriving global human community, we will have to attend to the massive inequalities that are part of our current social and economic arrangements. And we'll have to do it not just as a moral responsibility, but also because, deep in our interconnected guts, we know we can't be happy while others are suffering—especially if our own lifestyle choices contribute to that suffering. For those of us who have enough—or more likely an abundance—that attention will in most cases end up as a calling to live more simply as a practical sign of our human solidarity.

Finally, and ultimately, all of us human creatures share a God-given planet with myriad other plant and animal creatures and with the oceans, mountains, land, and air. God created and sustains them no less than us, and they, like us, are integral parts of this tapestry we call creation, the web of life. "When we try to pick out anything by itself," wrote the naturalist John Muir, long before the modern environmental consciousness was born, "we find it hitched to everything else in the Universe." Or as Pope Francis put it so succinctly and often in his encyclical *Laudato Si'*: "Everything is interconnected." This marvelous web is not only a thing of wonder and beauty, but also of physical necessity; our fates are linked with the fates of every other thing. We human creatures will only thrive to the extent our entire Earth thrives. And without rejecting the benefits of today's technologies or pretending that we can all "go native" and become hunter-gatherers again, I think simplicity offers us the chance to discern which elements of our modern life serve human and ecological well-being and which don't. That discernment, I believe, almost inevitably invites us to embrace choices that trade some of our material ambitions for a life that is more connected to, fed by, and nurturing of the natural world.

In part two, "Getting Practical," I'll explore with you several areas of our lives where a commitment to simplicity plays out: how we choose to deal with money, work, stuff, digital media; our dependence on others; travel, recreation, food choices; and finally (and most importantly), the way we show up and invest ourselves in the concentric circles of our relationships. I'm not planning on offering any recipes or specific roadmaps, but rather, I'll share some of my own discernment, struggles, and satisfaction in these areas in hopes that they may offer you some help as you navigate similar questions.

Again, thank you for taking the time to give your heart and mind to the spiritual and material journey of simplicity. I'm excited and grateful to walk through these pages with you, and I hope at the end of them, both of us will be even a little wiser for it.

••• part one •••

# WHY SIMPLICITY?

# one

# SIMPLE PLEASURES

D on't most of us want to be happy and fulfilled? That simple assumption, however, leads to a raft of complicated questions, which generally fall under two main headings. First, what are happiness and fulfillment really? Do we each define them differently, or are there common threads from person to person, across cultures, geography, and history? Second, however we might understand happiness and fulfillment, how do we get there? Again, is this different for each person, or are there any trustworthy guides or roadmaps?

One of my favorite sayings comes from St. Ireneaus, who claimed that the glory of God is the human being fully alive. For me, being "fully alive" is shorthand for being happy and fulfilled, and over the years I've reflected and journaled about the times when I felt most fully alive. It's a long and varied list. Many of these experiences have been in nature. In my twenties, I spent time solo-hiking parts of the Appalachian Trail, with all of my gear in a backpack and nothing but my own two feet to get me through the terrain. On those trips, I loved how everything was pared down to simple locomotion and the bare essentials of food, water, and shelter. Later, I would take up rock climbing, which requires an exquisite amount of focus and attention. One time, my climbing partners and I got stuck after dark on a Nevada mountaintop, and we had to make it through a chilly, sleepless night without adequate clothing, food, water, or shelter. Miserable as it was, I remember feeling utterly connected to my shivering partners and to the ancient mountain beneath me, whose roots go down deeper in time and space than I can imagine.

I've also had a lot of "fully alive" times that weren't about recreation, but about work. Every year for the last two decades, I have cut and split enough firewood to heat our home throughout each winter. I've spent countless hours tending orchards and planting, weeding, and harvesting gardens. Often, such times were an absolute grind of physical exhaustion, but plenty of times, I felt like I wouldn't want to be anywhere else or do anything else—especially when I've done those chores with my family. Aside from plain old hard physical work, there have also been plenty of occasions when I'm stumped by some sort of problem, like repairing a tractor or figuring out how to wire our home. But eventually, and often with the help of someone else, the issue gets resolved. I've faced similar conundrums—and solutions—in my work running a nonprofit organization, whether it's dealing with staff, financial challenges, or program delivery. And as a writer, I've often lost track of time altogether, wrestling with how to say the right thing in exactly the right way, because love of the craft demanded it of me and because I wanted to give my readers the fruit of those efforts. Like Jacob, I sometimes walk away from the struggle limping, but with soul-deep satisfaction at having stuck with it and finally been visited by the muse.

Hands down, though, marriage and parenting have presented some of the happiest (and hardest) moments of my life. From the magical moments of our courtship to the birth of our three children, there was no place I'd rather have been. From the high points of our kids' "firsts" to the everyday pleasures of evening meals and walks, Friday homemade pizza and Netflix nights, making music together, spending time with our extended family, and watching our kids grow into their own unique gifts, my best moments have been mediated by family. But it hasn't just been the rosy times. Like most couples, my wife and I have had difficult periods and tough conversations, and I've likewise had similar struggles with our kids, mostly because I can often be a blockhead of a husband and father. I'm not sure that "happy" and "fulfilled" are the right descriptors for those times of deep conflict, but when we eventually get through to the other side, the grace of forgiveness and reconciliation are deep and lasting gifts.

Several things strike me about these times when I have felt happiest and most fulfilled. For one, although I'm a person with strong religious commitments and regular spiritual practices, I have to admit that my deepest satisfactions have rarely come in moments of formal contemplative prayer or meditation, or during weekly Mass or even the high holy days. I think most of that is because unlike my wife, Cyndi, or St.

Francis, I haven't been gifted with a deeply affective spirituality. I have a more even baseline, which rarely dives deep into despair or vaults high into ecstasy. I get frustrated by this sometimes, and even cynical, but on the other hand, I don't expect or demand to see mystical visions of angels, so I don't tend to be too worried when my spiritual life feels a bit bland or dry. I do think, though, that having stayed relatively faithful to a prayer practice and to regular public worship has helped my heart open and my vision evolve. I can see more clearly and savor more deeply those moments when I notice how grace and love are at work in the world—and maybe even be more of an agent of grace and love myself. All that said, especially as I grow older, I do long for a deeper feeling of personal connection to God. In fact, part of the reason I'm writing this book is because when I look at someone like St. Francis, who was utterly beside himself with joy, I want to experience something like that level of trust and faith myself.

If my moments of deepest fulfillment aren't formally religious, plenty of other things aren't either. Almost all of them, for example, are low-tech. I'm grateful for my Kindle and (occasionally) my smartphone in a functional sort of way, but they have had next to nothing to do with my happiness. As we'll explore in a later chapter, technology, for all its benefits, can easily distract us from the "really real" that is the stuff of true meaning and satisfaction.

My best moments also haven't required a lot of money. I say that, but I also want to be careful here. I'll be the first to own the fact that I grew up and have remained comfortably middle class, and I've never had existential concerns about whether there would be food on the table or if the mortgage would get paid on time. That fact, which is certainly tied up with being a white, educated, physically and mentally healthy male, puts me in the absolute upper echelon compared to the vast majority of human beings who have ever lived. This fact has dogged me at every point of this book project because I feel like my experiences of and reflections about simplicity depend on a degree of privilege that is pretty much scandalous. I don't know any way around that other than to acknowledge it, take it seriously, and hope that it doesn't completely invalidate whatever I may write in these pages. After all, I assume that you, too, may come from a similar level of comfort—and frankly, we're the ones who really need to learn the practices of simplicity.

Even with all these caveats, though, I still stand by my main point: my peak moments generally have had little to do with spending much or any money. In almost every way, they have been moments that money simply can't buy, because they are tied to things that transcend prices and products and services. I think this is an important point to make at the outset of this book, so I'll belabor it. Money is essential to survival in the modern world, but the "economy" is not the be-all and end-all; it simply can't deliver on its promise to bring us joy and fulfillment. The best things in life really are free—or at least don't cost much.

My best moments have also had almost nothing to do with "winning" in the form of public recognition or beating others in some sort of competition—even though, I hate to admit, my personality is wired for achievement and praise. I've had some victories and accomplishments, though on a small scale compared to many. On those few occasions when I've garnered some sort of public praise, it has been something of a sugar high, which may have stoked my ego momentarily but ultimately felt insubstantial and fragile. I don't think I could build my house on that kind of shifting sand. The best gifts in this arena have come when some kind soul takes the time to reach out to me personally and lets me know that something I've done or written has brought about some real, helpful change in their life or thinking.

If my moments of deep satisfaction weren't necessarily brought about by formal religion, technology, money, or public accomplishment, what are the common threads in them? Most of the moments, timeless though they seemed, required time and attention. Much as I may have wanted to, I haven't found a way to schedule satisfying moments to happen in the free fifteen minutes I have between rushing from one activity to the next. I have to make an investment, to recognize for myself that what I am doing is deserving of my time and my undivided attention. You can't rush satisfaction, nor can you make it show up on demand. It's not efficient. It requires time in the woods, time at the blank page, time with friends and family, time spent honing your craft, time in quiet and stillness, time doing nothing. And yet I would never call this time "wasted."

I suspect that most of us, at least on some level, can tell when time is invested well or badly. I've watched plenty of Netflix shows that didn't really add much value to my life. On the other side of the coin, though, I've also spent countless hours with our young son, doing nothing but playing catch or Legos, and knowing that I could not possibly spend time better than that. If simplicity offers anything, it is the blessed assurance that our time has been well spent on things that matter, things that make our hearts glad.

My moments of satisfaction often have grown out of the devotion required to become skilled at something. My talents tend to be more broad than deep, and I tend to spread myself more thinly than I'd like, such that I don't invest the time and effort it would take to become exceptionally good at something. I have become decent at enough things to appreciate those who really shine in their chosen field. When it comes to writing, at least, I've generally been willing to take the time and make the effort required to fit words together just so and to sand and polish them until they shine. Writing isn't easy for me, and I've joked that I could be writing this book just as quickly with a chisel and stone tablet, given how slowly the words actually come to me and how endlessly I revise them. But when I see a sentence or a paragraph that says exactly what it needs to, with no waste or superfluity, in a way that is inviting and not pretentious, it's worth it. I would never claim mastery, but I'm grateful to experience some rare writing moments when I'm in flow. Those experiences lead me to marvel at (and if I'm honest, sometimes to envy) those who really have become masters of their craft, whatever that craft is. I revere the devoted mother, the skilled carpenter, the brilliant scientist or famous poet, and everyone in between who have given themselves fully to the development of their passion and skill for a chosen vocation, with all of the discipline, grit, and sacrifice it requires of them.

A fundamental component of my most satisfying experiences has been *connection*—to others, to the natural world, to my deepest and truest self, and through all these things, ultimately to God. Most of the time, these connections have been brimful of obvious pleasure—the great conversation, the warm feelings that come when friends and family are gathered in love, those times when I feel that human beings are simply amazing creatures and I'm glad to be part of the human family. But sometimes those connections are difficult. Certainly, when I encounter news reports on genocide, sex trafficking, and other atrocities committed across the globe, I feel shame at being part of the human race. How in the world can we be so cruel to one another? Closer to home—at home, in fact—my wife and I have had challenging times together, times when we have come to the limits of our own relationship skills and ability to forgive. Then, somehow, we are carried through by honesty, love, grace, and the mysterious power of the marriage sacrament. I've had similar kinds of experiences with our kids, and to a lesser degree with friends, other family members, and coworkers. It's hard to describe such bruising journeys in terms of pleasure or satisfaction. But there's something undeniably real and authentic about them, and I end up feeling that another hard-won stitch has been sewn in the garment of our common humanity. We come back to the deep truth that we belong to one another, that we are part and parcel of one another, that one of us cannot be without the other's existence. *Ubuntu*, as they say in Africa: "I am because we are."

The satisfactions of connection in the natural world have two sides to them as well. I've been blessed to witness huge, gorgeous, inspiring natural landscapes that are worthy of the psalmists' praise. Likewise, having spent many, many hours in the woods, I've watched the graceful, silent flight of an owl, the loping of a red fox, and the meandering of deer, raccoons, opossums, wild turkeys, and other creatures as they move past me, their fellow creature. I've seen nature at her best and most beautiful, on her own terms, and although such experiences were not for my sake, I've felt a part of that wonder.

On the other hand, I've borne the unforgiving chill of winter; I've worked out in the merciless heat and humidity of high summer; and I've witnessed flood and wind and rain and other natural phenomena that remind me how small and expendable I am, hitched to this untamably wild beast we call the natural world. Some of the satisfactions of connection are hard-won by physical suffering at nature's hand. And, of course, I feel deep grief in knowing how much nature has been suffering at our hand, with our reckless disregard for the health and beauty of Earth's ecosystems. Even though I've tried to cultivate a meaningful relationship to the rest of the natural world, I also regret that my connection is radically impoverished compared to the abilities of my human ancestors (and some indigenous peoples today), whose very lives depended on being able to read the book of nature with skill and fluency. I long for closer ties.

What binds these experiences of pleasure and satisfaction together? In some cases, it has felt so good to know that I'm being of service to something greater than myself: that I'm giving my best to the people I care about, to the work that is mine to do in the world, to the good of the human family and the creation. Each of us, I believe, is called to give something special to the world and to become our truest self in the offering of it. The ability to do so is a great gift, divinely given. In other instances, I've been the recipient of the largesse of human kindness, or I've beheld the beauty of the natural world, freely given—and in it all, I've been pulled out of my small, cramped, ego-self into the gift of a greater, more beautiful, more blessed belonging.

That's it, really. There may be various aspects and nuances to the pleasures and satisfactions of simplicity, which we can explore together throughout this book. But in the end, the greatest pleasure isn't having all our ego-needs met, but instead being drawn out of our ego into a wider world of belonging. We may work to cultivate this kind of self-transcendence, but it is always and ultimately a gift: a gift from others, from brother sun and sister moon and the rest of the created world, and in and through all of these, from the Creator and Giver of all gifts.

# two

# LETTING GO

Upon sprouting or being born or hatched, pretty much all living things grow. It's a basic biological principle that creatures start off small and build up size and strength—some with amazing rapidity, and others, like an oak or redwood or saguaro cactus, with the slow patience of decades and centuries. I remember when our twin girls were born, at around five pounds each, I could easily hold one in each palm. It was hard to believe that human creatures could be so small, and although they were absolutely adorable in their tininess, we were eager for them to put on weight.

As Eva and Clare grew, we thanked God and rejoiced at every outfit that no longer fit, every height mark scribed on the pantry door frame. We also reveled in all of the other milestones of growth: first words, first steps, learning to read, and entering school. We were a little less thrilled at their tendency to amass things, as our house began to bulge with stuffed animals (thanks, grandparents!), My Little Ponies, Schleich animals, and other toys and knick-knacks. In closets, under beds, and behind couches, we would find piles of hoarded objects, which sometimes included grapes that had long since turned to raisins and old pieces of cheese that had turned into something I'd rather not describe.

Our girls have since become young women and now have relatively little interest in stuff. But they are voracious readers and inquisitive, thoughtful learners, and we are thrilled to watch them gain knowledge and experience, form opinions, and maybe, just maybe, reach their goal of becoming taller than 5'1". I'm excited to see them journey into their adulthood as they continue their education, take up work that calls them, and perhaps become wives and mothers. Who knows what new gifts they might bring into the world?

As with growing individuals, so also it is with collectives. Any population of creatures that has inadequate numbers risks extinction, so all creatures have an innate drive not only to grow as individuals, but also to reproduce and so expand the collective, whether it's a forest or a school of fish or a human population. And as our human numbers grow, our systems need to grow as well; more people require a larger economy, more governmental and legal structures, more extensive agriculture, and so forth.

In other words, growth is good. But only up to a point.

What we're witnessing now, on both individual and collective levels, is growth run amok, growth gone unchecked, growth beyond proper limits. On the individual level, that looks like obesity, income inequality, overconsumption, personal debt, and the various diseases of affluence. On the collective level, it looks like systems and structures that have become dysfunctional: an economy whose growth depends on underpaid labor and is consuming our one habitable planet, a government that ignores those in need and invests huge amounts of resources in protecting and projecting its power. We know how this story ends: badly. The Roman Empire took a similar course centuries ago. It grew through conquest and enslavement, and because its growth was malignant—using up people and the natural resources of grain fields and forests—it eventually collapsed under its own weight.

Growth is necessary, but healthy growth always stays within proper boundaries and limits. This is the careful balance that keeps human beings, human societies, and entire ecosystems healthy. As much as I wanted our daughters to grow like weeds at age two, I wouldn't want the same for them at age twenty-two.

If growth is one element of flourishing, and proper limits to growth another, there is a third: loss, decay, and diminishment. Life grows, abides, and then recedes, giving way to new forms of life. However cruel we may find it, this seems to be the divinely designed eternal cycle of the world. It seems to hold true for individuals, communities, entire ecosystems and, though it is more difficult and dreadful to fathom, for our planet, solar system, and galaxy—perhaps even for the entire universe.

This idea of loss and diminishment is especially hard to swallow for the materially rich Western nations. One of our strong cultural stories is that if we amass enough wealth and possessions and accomplishments and experiences, if we eat enough organic food and get enough exercise, if we calibrate our life just right, we can somehow insulate ourselves from tragedy and loss. The only loss that we can admit into this pipedream is excess weight. But I suspect that the amount of resources our market- and advertising-driven culture invests to prop up such a fiction is just a sign of how tenuous the fiction really is. Who really believes, at least at 2:00 a.m. on a sleepless night, that we can get out of here unscathed, that we can get a free pass on loss? It's the common denominator of human existence. Even though I've enjoyed almost unbelievably good fortune for almost a half-century, I've still had to contend with the loss of family stability due to divorce, the loss of my dear grandfather to suicide, and several severe physical injuries that have left indelible marks on me. None of us—*none* of us—can get around loss, if only the loss of our parents in their time and ultimately the loss of our own life.

The question shouldn't be how to minimize or avoid loss. It's not possible, and by trying, we just end up making our life small, unhappy, and inconsequential. The real question is how to make room for loss in our life, with true awareness and intention—even to make friends with it, to the extent that's possible. In our various ways, each one of us has been faced with that invitation because of the COVID-19 pandemic. At the very least, making room for loss means greeting it with an open heart and making the best use of it when it casts its dark, uninvited shadow across our doorstep. When Nelson Mandela lost twenty-seven years of his freedom, sitting in a South African prison, he had every right to become bitter and resentful. And yet he came out of prison not tallying his losses, but full of the focus, energy, and passion he needed to lead a nation into a new, post-apartheid future. If you think about the wise, admirable people in your life—whether those you have known personally or those who have spoken to you from the public stage or books or history—I would wager that a common element of their stories is how they were transformed by suffering some significant loss.

Authentic spirituality requires that we allow ourselves to be transformed: to have our entire being opened to a world far larger than the confines of our own ego, such that we appreciate the (sometimes terrible and frightening) beauty of that larger world, recognize our belonging in it, and make moral commitments to serve this larger life of which we are a part. The great spiritual masters seem to agree that this process of transformation is almost never a process of addition. It almost always entails losing or letting go of things. Jesus didn't promise his early disciples a life of luxury and ease. Instead, he told them they would have to let go of pretty much everything in order to follow him. The early monastics pared their life down to the barest of essentials out in the deserts of Egypt and Syria. Beloved St. Francis of Assisi let go of his prospects as a middle-class Italian cloth merchant and pledged his allegiance to Lady Poverty instead.

Why? Why does letting go seem to be such a necessary element in the equation of transformational spirituality? One answer is as simple as it is painful: because if life inevitably entails loss, and if true spirituality is about fully embracing the (often messy) reality of life, then any authentic spiritual path must make room for loss. Otherwise, spirituality really is just an opiate for the masses or a form of bypass, leading us away from life's mystery rather than into the heart of it. In some sense, letting go of things voluntarily, as a spiritual practice, ends up being good training for those inevitable times when life *demands* that we let go—of material possessions, relationships, jobs, health, and so forth. Being able to let go gracefully rather than grasp on greedily is a hallmark of spiritual maturity.

There's another answer, though, which is one of the core themes of this book. I believe that all of us are born with the image of God stamped indelibly into the fibers of our being. Despite our personal flaws and the brokenness of our institutions, we all have divine wisdom and goodness inscribed on our hearts. We don't acquire it from without as much as we uncover it from within. Unfortunately, though, our personal experiences and cultural messages tend to have us believe that our worthiness resides in something external, something we can cultivate, achieve, amass, or purchase. This is a lie, an illusion, which obscures the divine goodness that is the birthright of each one of us. We see through a glass dimly. An important part of spiritual practice, then, is "cleaning the lens": letting go of the layers of illusion piled up by the ego, which helps us to rediscover the deepest truths of who we are, what the world is, and how we belong.

"Cleaning the lens" to discover and affirm our authentic selves sounds well and good, and I'm confident that most spiritual traditions and teachers would agree with that idea, at least in principle. But there's a vast difference between principle and practice. Simply holding up the principle isn't nearly enough, because it has to become real in the external realities of our daily actions and choices. Most of us can usually tell when there is dissonance between what people profess and what they live out in practice. Perhaps this is why we seem to relish the downfall of evangelical preachers who rail against fornication but are later found to be promiscuous, or self-help gurus who milk donations from fervent followers and are then exposed for financial misdeeds. We all struggle with some degree of hypocrisy, of course. But word and deed, even if they aren't completely in unison, at least need to sing harmony with one another. So how, in real terms, do we live in such a way that we are always letting go of what is unhelpful so we can keep our vision clear and claim the truth of our core goodness and belonging?

In some ways, the rest of this book is an attempt to reflect on that question. For now, I'd like to reflect in somewhat general terms, knowing that we'll be doing plenty of unpacking in the chapters to come.

When I was a young man, I was fascinated by theology and philosophy, and I couldn't read enough of it. Not for a moment do I regret the thousands of pages I have digested of great minds reflecting on spiritual truths. They have helped—and still do help—establish some of my fundamental beliefs about God, myself, and the world. But along with this wonderful learning came the temptation to believe that gaining spiritual wisdom was a process of accreting ideas, concepts, beliefs, doctrines, and dogmas, as well as saying plenty of prayers and performing plenty of religious devotions. See how even the language of "gaining" wisdom smacks of an acquisitive mindset, as if one becomes holy or enlightened by amassing such intangibles? According to this mindset, the sage is the one who has acquired the most insight, and who, if you're one of the blessed, might deign to dispense it to you.

But do you sense how wrong that feels? It makes spiritual wisdom the property (there's that language again) of the elite, those who have learned more and better and longer than you or I have, who have had more experiences, attended more retreats and conferences, and so forth. It consigns most of us to feeling like second-class plebeians.

The real spiritual masters, in my opinion, are the ones who have been able and willing to let go of *anything* they might cling to before God—even their theological certainties. They talk less about knowing *about* God, or even *knowing* God, and more about *being known by* God—a God they experience well beyond the boundaries of their knowledge and understanding. These are folks like John of the Cross, whose dark night of the soul undid most of what he thought he was sure of, or Meister Eckhart, who prayed that God rid him of God, because any conception of God he might have would not possibly be adequate. These are folks like St. Thomas Aquinas, who filled volumes with systematic theology and then, near the end of his life, had a vision that made all of what he'd written seem like straw to him, such that he left his great *Summa* unfinished. The moral I take from such figures is that wisdom is as much "unknowing" as anything else: letting go of, or at least holding on less tightly to, everything we thought we knew. Isn't this fundamentally the example of Jesus, too, who finally let go and was stripped of everything, who moaned on the Cross that even God had forsaken him?

For me, these examples of holy wisdom haven't led me to give up reading or learning, whether about spiritual matters or anything else. Old habits die hard, and I wouldn't even want them to die. But at least on my good days, I expect less and less to find the answers "out there" somewhere. I'm more willing to dwell in the cloud of unknowing, more willing and able to let myself be surprised by God "doing a new thing," as Isaiah and the other prophets preached.

There's a paradox here. On the one hand, I feel a lot less sure about a lot of things than I did earlier in my life, and that's pretty unsettling. On the other hand, it's a tremendous relief not to need to know everything, not to have everything figured out, but instead to be able to trust in the mystery of life and the mystery of God. The Buddhists call this "beginner's mind." I like to call it humility—intellectual, spiritual, and personal.

Humility is, in my opinion, the hallmark spiritual virtue of letting go. It's an open-minded, openhearted, openhanded way to move through the world. To be humble is to make room for life as it comes, without the need to grasp too tightly, even (and especially) to certainty. This kind of attitude is what keeps your vision from clouding up and occluding. No one manages this perfectly, of course. That's why life seems all too willing to deal us periodic humiliations that knock down our towers of Babel and drop us back onto the ground of our being: the truth that we are held in divine and loving hands, without being able to do anything to deserve or ruin it. In other words, the spirituality of letting go, or beginner's mind, or humility, or however you want to describe it, is ultimately a way of believing and living that reminds us at every turn that it's about realities far larger, deeper, more mysterious, and more wonderful than ourselves.

# three

# FOR THE LOVE OF THE POOR

grew up comfortably middle-class in a suburb outside of a small town. I didn't have much direct contact with poverty until I lived in Atlanta during graduate school at Emory University. Like many large cities—especially large Southern cities—Atlanta has socioeconomic divides that generally fall along racial lines. Though I landed in the well-to-do part of Atlanta that surrounds Emory, eventually I got connected with Holy Comforter Episcopal Church, a small mission parish in a rundown part of south Atlanta. Holy Comforter's parishioners were—and still are—mainly poor people with mental and physical disabilities. As I became more involved, twice a week I would drive one of the church's old vans to pick up many of the parishioners from local group care homes, and I helped serve Wednesday evening and Sunday meals. For a year, I even lived on the church property in a small basement apartment. In all of this, I got to know these parishioners very well.

Something profound and beautiful happened to me during those years. I, who had always been eager to impress and please others with my intellect and my accomplishments, found myself in a situation where these things had no currency whatsoever. I couldn't hide behind them, and so my encounters with the parishioners had an amazing transparency to them that I've rarely found since. I encountered something at Holy Comforter that was *real*, and so I was able to become more real as well. My experience there was more spiritually formative for me than almost all of my fancy graduate theological education.

And what did *real* mean? When I lived in the church basement, real meant sometimes getting tired of mentally ill and addicted parishioners banging on my door at all hours. It often meant wishing that they were cleaner, smelled better, and sang more on key. Real also meant having my heart broken many times by the pain I encountered among my friends at Holy Comforter. Real meant anger and frustration with a social support system that consistently failed to provide them what simple human dignity would require. But real also meant seeing through the fundamental lie of our culture: the belief that we are separate and self-sufficient. When you're poor, it's hard to deny that you need help. For better and for worse, you have to depend on others. The Christian tradition claims that God has a special affection for those who are poor, and Jesus gravitated toward the poor and powerless in his ministry. At Holy Comforter, the reason for this became clear to me. Poverty, for all that is miserable and unjust about it, gives the lie to the acquisition arms race that is our culture.

What ends up counting most is not socioeconomic status, but connection, relationship, love, and openheartedness.

Since my experience at Holy Comforter, I've lived with the question of how to make room for the poor in my heart, in my thinking about how we can co-create a flourishing world, and in my efforts to bring about that world. I come back to three main convictions: friendship, solidarity, and service.

## FRIENDSHIP WITH THE POOR

Friendship with people who are poor is exactly what I experienced at Holy Comforter: real contact and relationships, with all of their challenges. When I was at Holy Comforter, I didn't encounter "the poor" in the abstract, but I got to know John, Billy, Annie, James, and many others. Whenever I would pick her up from her group home, Annie, an older Black woman, would look at me with her clouded, half-blind eyes and assure me, "I'm prayin' for ya." And I prayed for her too. Different as they were, her world and my world intersected, and I think we were both the better for it. I cared about Annie, and she cared about me. I knew, in an agonizing way, how Billy's anger issues—and his unfortunate habit of impersonating a law enforcement officer—often got him in trouble with the actual police. When I was in a graduate seminar, discussing some abstract theological point, I would often filter my academic learning through my relationships with my friends at Holy Comforter. How would this or that idea land with James or Carol? Could they make any sense of it at all? Would it have any meaning for them? Did it or could it take account of their lives, their gifts, their needs?

Since that special time as a young man, I've not had such regular daily contact with people who are poor. That separation is a common and understandable phenomenon of a comfortable, middle-class life and a professional career, but I think it's unfortunate, and I continue to discern how I might make room for friendships in my life that cross socioeconomic boundaries. I think often about how intentional communities like Sant'Egidio, L'Arche, and The Catholic Worker have put friendship with poor people at the center of their common life. I am beginning to believe that the best way to be friends with people who are poor is to be in some form of community—whether that's a conventional house of worship or another kind of organization—that has explicit commitments to cultivating such relationships. You may have the level of motivation that enables you to build those kinds of relationships on your own, but for me, who can so easily be swept up in the momentum of my own concerns, having the support and challenge of similarly committed others is probably the only way I'll be able to seek out and sustain real relationships with people who are poor.

## SOLIDARITY WITH THE POOR

Regardless of our particular friendships with poor people, I think all of us are called to be in solidarity with them. This is especially important because in a world of such massive inequality, there are so, so many people who are poor, almost all of whom you'll never get a chance to meet. The world's "bottom billion" are so desperately poor that they can't secure their basic needs. Another billion teeters on the edge of extreme poverty: just one illness, lost job, or other disruption away from joining the bottom billion. Even in a developed nation like America, 40 percent of our population—over 130 million souls—couldn't manage an unexpected four hundred dollar expense. The wealth inequality in our country is staggering: just three individuals—Microsoft's Bill Gates, Amazon's Jeff Bezos, and investor Warren Buffet—have more wealth than the bottom 50 percent of all Americans put together, and the top 1 percent of Americans have more than the bottom 90 percent put together. Even having sat with those figures for a while now, I still have trouble fathoming them.

In the face of such crushing realities, it's easy to reach for "shoulds." The rich should be less acquisitive. They should be more generous to others. Our laws and economic policies should prevent such accumulation of power and wealth in the first place, so that we have a more equal society.

A lot of activism and moral reform relies heavily on "shoulds." I certainly don't discount the need to call out greed, corruption, and inequality and to point fingers at culprits. But while this kind of motivation is necessary, it will never be sufficient fuel for long-term behavioral change at the level of individuals or of an entire society. If solving inequality— or any other personal or social problem—were as simple as articulating clear shoulds (and shouldn'ts) and then investing a lot of willpower behind them, don't you think that would have worked by now?

So as I consider what it means to be in solidarity with those who are poor, I'm less inclined to be preachy and more inclined to be curious. I find myself wondering: What does it feel like to have so much money in the face of so much poverty, especially in the face of the radical poverty of those who lack even the basic necessities of sufficient food, safe drinking water, and sanitation?

It's not as big an imaginative leap as you may think. When I was learning about income inequality and "the 1 percent," I came across some information that made it a lot harder just to point fingers at rich folks like Buffet, Bezos, and Gates. Because when you broaden the focus to include the entire human population, the picture looks very different. According to the Global Rich List, if you earn at least $32,400 a year, you are part of the richest 1 percent of the world population. So even with my moderate middle-class income, I'm part of the 1 percent—and so probably are you. My family and I may not have an extravagant lifestyle, but we are well insulated from any existential concern about lacking enough food, losing our home, or being unable to ensure a decent educa-tion for our children. Although I have always worked hard to earn my living, I know that I couldn't be where I am without the benefit of a lot of baked-in privilege that goes with being a middle-class, educated white male who grew up in a mostly nurturing, mostly stable home environment.

So I ask you as I ask myself: How does it feel to know that so many members of the human family have so much less than we do—and that in many cases, our affluence has contributed to their poverty? How does this feel in your heart? How does this feel in your body? If you're like me, you don't need a lot of elaborate statistics to know that there are billions of people who are suffering crushing poverty at this very moment. If you start to pay attention, you feel this inside yourself. We may often distract ourselves or deny it, but there's no getting around the fact that we are connected in more ways and to a greater extent than we can ever fathom. The deeper we go in our spiritual practice, the more obvious and undeniable these connections become.

Often these connections are painful. When I really sit with these glaring inequalities, my heart hurts. Honestly, I wonder whether we're so hard on so-called rich people because we want to scapegoat them so we don't have to feel the pain of acknowledging our own privilege in the face of so much poverty. And whether or not that's true, I'm absolutely sure that most of us, on a daily basis, find ways to anaesthetize ourselves from feeling that pain as acutely or as often as we otherwise might. I know that I do. I wrap myself up in the daily concerns of my job, my family, and my health. I distract myself with reading, entertainment, hobbies, and exercise. And why not? If I really let all that misery in on a daily basis, it would overwhelm me.

If we can let in the pain and grief of such inequality and suffering, however, we have a firm foundation for our solidarity. It doesn't depend on willpower, guilt, or shame, but on knowing with all our heart and soul and mind that in our global human family, we all belong to one another, and so we will only flourish when all of us flourish. And the joy we can feel in such connections will be thick and strong enough to hold us all.

## IN SERVICE TO THE POOR

Solidarity with the poor isn't just a feeling, whether of grief or joy or both. If it is true, soul-deep solidarity, it will lead to action. It will affect how we spend our money and our time, our choices about lifestyle and various forms of civic engagement, from voting to protesting. For some of us, it may be concrete acts of service in direct connection with people who are poor, such as working at a shelter or a food bank. For others, it may mean supporting organizations that do direct service work in our stead.

If you do such service out of the wrong motivations, it will generally end up bolstering your own ego, or being patronizing and demeaning to those you serve. But real solidarity has connection and humility hardwired into it, which help keep those dynamics in check. In the end, you'll almost certainly end up being transformed. I see that regularly in the nonprofit I run, which does a lot of work to bring the tools and benefits of mindfulness to underserved members of the Louisville community. We do this mainly through a corps of volunteers who have a strong meditation practice and have been trained to provide basic mindfulness instruction for adults and at-risk kids who are clients of the social service organizations with which we partner. Even though I'm not involved directly (the curse of being an organizational leader is often empowering others to do good work rather than doing it yourself), I love hearing from those who are doing this teaching and mentoring. They have seen powerful changes in their clients, who use the mindfulness tools they learn to deal with addictions, manage the stresses of their poverty, and avoid escalating violent situations. Our teachers have seen powerful changes in themselves too. Their hearts are broken open and they have ever-stronger convictions about being of service.

Whatever our own form of service, this kind of transformation is possible for all of us.

## FOR THE LOVE OF THE POOR

Being present to the poor through friendship, solidarity, and service isn't just a helpful set of moral principles. It's a virtuous circle, with each feeding and amplifying the others, and all leading to a more authentic way of being in the world. Because when we make room for these in our life, we're making room for love, the common bond that can bridge any gulf poverty may create.

# four

# FOR THE LOVE OF THE EARTH

et's start with a simple fact: any material thing we have or eat or use has been taken from the Earth. Your shoes, my eyeglasses, your big screen TV or Big Mac, my collection of power tools—they all came from something that grew in the soil or the sea, or else their materials were mined from the Earth itself in the form of ores, minerals, or fossil fuels. Everything. Here's a second fact: unlike in nature, where every single thing gets recycled in some form or fashion, in modern industrial economies, 90 percent of what we take from the Earth ends up as refuse and pollution. If you don't get those two truths, nothing else in this chapter is going to make sense to you.

Given that the basic functioning of our planet is breaking down because of those two facts, two conclusions seem pretty clear to me. The first is huge, structural, and systemic: we, collectively, have to figure out a way for our economy to become circular and conserving rather than linear and wasteful, since this is the only way we can have healthy humans and a flourishing world rather than a strip mine and a sewer. We have to do all that is within our power to demand and advocate for those kinds of changes. The second is deeply personal and connects to the central theme of this book: we all have to find ways to participate less in this destructive machine, and simplifying our lives is an important way to achieve that.

When I first was planning this chapter and figuring out a way to advocate for those two conclusions, I plotted out a tightly argued essay demonstrating the necessity of adopting a simpler lifestyle, which entails using fewer resources and less energy so that we could all help promote and protect the flourishing of our planet. I was going to make a strong moral case from the Christian tradition, arguing that the Earth belongs to God, not to us, and we have a duty and vocation to steward it well and to care for the lives of God's creatures, human and nonhuman. I was going to point out that the Earth is sacramental; it is a source of beauty, inspiration, and revelation. To the extent we damage and degrade it, we are impoverishing our own creative and religious imagination. Finally, I was going to play the self-preservation card. If we continue to degrade the health and resilience of the Earth's ecological systems, we will commit suicide as a species, bringing many other species over the precipice with us.

All of those arguments, I believe, are true. But now that I'm actually writing this chapter, I realize that I was on the wrong track in my planning. I know very few people who have ever changed their behavior in any significant and lasting way simply as a result of a well-organized, logical argument. We might like to think we're rational creatures, but for the most part, we really aren't.

Real, lasting behavioral change tends to come from some profound personal experience. My Aunt Jane, for example, crusades tirelessly to end breast cancer because she has survived it herself and is deeply woven into a network of fellow cancer survivors. A friend of mine raises hundreds of thousands of dollars every year in his spare time from running his own marketing company to find a cure for cystic fibrosis, which afflicts his son.

These powerful experiences can be ones of fear, pain, or suffering. Decades ago, I sustained an awful injury while sliding down a stair banister, and I've never even been tempted to slide down another. I recently suffered a serious, surgery-and-rehab-requiring knee injury as a result of a diving accident at a local pool, and I will likely choose never to climb onto a diving board again. This kind of direct experience is far more effective at motivating behavioral change than, say, the abstract fear of having heart trouble or diabetes fifteen years from now, or having an uninhabitable global climate several decades hence. Relying on such immediate negative experiences to bring about personal and collective change, however, can be very problematic, especially when it comes to environmental issues. One problem is obvious: Wouldn't it be better to avoid such unpleasant experiences when possible? Why learn money management skills by suffering through a bankruptcy? Along similar lines, the nature of environmental damage is such that by the time you're really suffering, much of what is causing it is irreversible—as with species extinction and soil erosion—and could even hit a tipping point and become exponentially worse, as in the vicious cycle feedback loops we face in a warming climate. Another problem is that when you are operating out of fear, pain, or suffering, your instinctual lizard brain tends to kick in, and it's more likely that you'll make poor decisions about the best and most skillful choice of behavior.

I've spent almost three decades advocating for care of the Earth, and while in some ways my understanding of the various issues has become much more nuanced in the most important ways, it has become much simpler. My ethic is as simple as this: if we cease and desist from making our planet uninhabitable for us and many other species, if we finally choose to tend this creation with skill and care, it will be because we are moved by the world's beauty, awed by its complex interrelatedness, and feel ourselves kin with the rest of creation. Put simply, because we experience a great love for the world. What we love is what moves our heart, and what moves our heart is what moves our lives.

Although the analogy isn't perfect, the best way I can illustrate this is by talking about our children. Why, over the past seventeen years, have my wife and I invested so much time, energy, money, and concern for our three children? It's not just the biological drive to perpetuate our genes. Anyone who has been a parent—especially an adoptive parent—knows that this is an utterly inadequate answer. It's not just some hope that they will take care of us in our old age. If that were the driving concern, we'd have skipped having kids and put all the money we would have saved into our retirement accounts and long-term care insurance. It's not just social pressure and convention. It's not fear that if we neglect them, someone will turn us in to the CPS.

No. All of those may be motivating factors to some degree, but the simple answer is love. We care for our children because we love them. We care for our children because in our love for them, we realize that they are unique, amazing creatures—even our identical twin daughters, who had different personalities right from the start. We care for our children because in the eyes of our love, they are beautiful, inside and out. We care for our children because in our love for them, we wonder at the people they are, and we hope for the people they are becoming. We care for our children even though they may break our heart—and in each breaking, our heart grows larger and more capable of care. Our love creates and preserves the best in them and the best in us.

Granted, there are some parents who do not love their children. And none of us loves our children as well as they deserve or as well as we might wish, whether because of our own personal difficulties or the mere fact of being fallible human beings. We live in a culture that often makes it difficult to be a loving and attentive parent. But by and large, that we would love our children seems good and natural to us. How, then, might we cultivate a similar kind of love for the rest of the natural world?

Let me stick a little longer with the analogy of raising children. For those of us who have biological children, we have a built-in bond with them, because they are literally the flesh of our flesh. I look at my daughters, and they have my hands.

I look at my son, and he has my stubborn, cowlicky hair. However alienated we may get from one another, biological parents have a connection with our children that goes right down into the base pairs of our DNA. The same is true with our connection to the rest of the natural world. As the Genesis creation story points to so poetically, we are literally made up of the Earth—every molecule of our being ultimately came from the Earth. We are children of Earth, flesh of the Earth's flesh and bone of her bone. We are not some aliens that fate dropped onto this planet to make shift. We human animals are native to this place and have coevolved with the Earth for millions of years. We may have isolated and insulated ourselves with technology, but deep in our collective psyche, deep in our instinctual drives and our inherited knowledge, we know that we belong. True, it can sometimes be a contentious relationship. The Earth can be cruel and unforgiving, and survival can be a struggle. But it is the struggle of family, not contention between strangers.

All parents, whether biological or adoptive, have a spiritual connection with their children. Again, we can ignore it, deny it, be deaf and blind to it, and fail to live up to it, but I would wager that almost any parent reading this book would agree that by whatever mysterious mechanisms, our bond with our kids goes far beyond the merely material. Even if we can't necessarily measure and understand these connections, we nonetheless know them to be real. So it is also with our connection to the rest of the Earth. We are, as Thomas Berry once wrote, a "single, sacred community" with the entire human and nonhuman community of Earth because we all share a common divine source and sustenance. Why else would it be so common that for so many of us, our profound spiritual experiences entail an encounter with nature? Like knows like. We resonate with the Earth because the same Holy Spirit that breathes life into us breathes the same life into all of creation. All of us—human and nonhuman—are children of the same loving, living God. We are all siblings; as St. Francis put it, the sun is our brother and the moon is our sister.

Before we cue the theme song from *The Lion King*, though, I think it's important not to be overly romantic or dreamy about these relationships. We may be kin with all of creation, but let's face it: family life is often difficult and painful. I love my wife and kids dearly and deeply, and for exactly that reason, I have wounded them and been wounded by them more than anyone else on the planet. And that's in a decently functional family. Plenty of other families, including my own family of origin, fall far short even of that. Love is complicated. Love can be painful. And in spite of this—or I would say *because* of this—love is still the best and perhaps only path to becoming fully and truly alive. This is as true for our relationship with the rest of creation as it is for our relationship with our family members.

So I return to my question: How do we cultivate our love for the Earth? It's a start to acknowledge that we are material and spiritual kin. But there is one simple way to grow in our love for the Earth, and it has nothing (at least directly) to do with recycling, reducing our carbon footprint, going vegan, or any of the other things on our "be a good environmentalist" aspirational checklist. It's the exact same thing you would do to tend the love you have for your spouse, your parent, or your child: simply spend time with the rest of creation, on its own terms and without a particular agenda.

When you think about it, this is so basic as to be self-explanatory. And yet so few of us do this well—including me. When we lived on a farm, I was often outside, but so much of the time, it was with a task to do: planting, tending, and harvesting gardens and fruit trees, cutting hay or timber or firewood, exercising. It was far rarer for me to be outside simply enjoying the natural world. Whenever we took walks in our woods, my wife and kids would often—and rightfully—chide me for comments I would make about which trees I needed to cut. In fact, we often tussled over several trees on our property that were damaged by lightning or by another tree falling on them—misshapen, contorted trees that would never end up making good timber, or good firewood, or even living out their full lives. I couldn't see the use of keeping them and wanted to take them down to make room for other trees that had a better shot. Why should these suboptimal trees take up sunlight, water, and soil nutrients that other trees, which had better chances, could use? My family, however, seemed to have special love for these misfit trees, and they complained of my ruthless practicality. Couldn't I see the beauty in a tree that had been bent over 90 degrees but had refused to die, such that it was sending up a line of new trunks straight out of the fallen one? Couldn't I appreciate a malformed tree as a beautiful, stubborn defiance of death and, for that matter, of human intentions? Couldn't I step out of woodlot manager mode long enough to greet the trees as fellow creatures of the

Creator, to sense their own spiritual value even in brokenness—to see, as William Blake did, the angels perching in their branches?

I imagine it will take me longer than the rest of my life truly to meet the world as its own subject rather than as the object of my own plans and priorities. But slowly, slowly, I'm learning. Thank goodness nature has such patience! Whenever I take a meandering walk, or watch the hummingbirds at our feeder, or just sit under the trees on our front lawn, feeling the Earth beneath me and the breeze on my skin, I feel that my own roots are growing deeper, intertwining with those of the trees, and all seeking a common Source: the divine power that holds everything together. The more time I spend, agendaless, in and with the rest of nature, the broader and deeper grows my sense of connection, my sense of kinship, the feelings of love and the commitments of love. Though native to us, that bond must be nurtured, and its primary nutrient is time. Time is the good soil in which relationships grow and flower. Time, given with presence rather than preoccupation, is the greatest gift. There is no substitute.

But if I am always hundreds of emails in the hole, if I am always running to catch up with my life, if I am so often bullied and tormented by the clock and the calendar, how in the world is it possible to find the time to spend in nature? "Finding" the time doesn't seem like the right analogy, as if time were coquettishly playing hide-and-seek. Decades ago, I visited Petra, Jordan, and saw the incredible stone buildings that were literally carved into the side of a mountain. *That* is how I sometimes feel about making time to spend connecting with nature. How might it be possible to make room for a friendlier relationship with time so it really feels like the gift it is rather than something carved out with a hammer and chisel? How might it be possible not only to be in nature, but to be there with unhurried presence, with wonder, gratitude, and in and through all these things, with patience?

The answer to that question—or rather, an exploration of that question—is what drives the rest of this book. In the chapters that follow, I'd like to ponder with you in much more specific and practical ways how we might recover the sort of *kairos*-time spaciousness that would enable such a relationship with nature to flourish. How might our lives become simple enough to sing harmony with the song of the scarlet tanager, with the centuries-old oak, and in and through these, with their and our Creator?

• • • part two • • •

# GETTING PRACTICAL

I f simplicity is going to be something more than an abstract concept or feel-good idea, we're actually going to have to do something about it. It's going to have to change the way we make decisions and the way we act. "You will know them by their fruits" (Matthew 7:16). The process of simplifying your life in a way that is true to the Gospel, true to your own personality, and true to your individual circumstances will look different for you than it does for me. But there are some common themes and situations. In the remainder of this book, we'll look at the commonplace areas of life to see how a commitment to the values of simplicity can be lived out in our everyday existence.

# five

# MONEY

W hy not start with the hard stuff first? Since money is one of the primary ways we engage with the world, money can bring out the best and the worst in us—our addictions, insecurities, and moral failings, but also our integrity, generosity, and freedom. Because money is such a ubiquitous part of our lives and can be such a stumbling block, it's also one of the most powerful opportunities we have to live out (or at least, to live toward) our fundamental values. Dealing well with money can help us cultivate true wealth and freedom, become the kind of people we want to be, and create the kind of world—socially and environmentally—that we want to see.

All that said, I feel as though I need to open this chapter by acknowledging that perhaps more than anything else I've written about in this book, dealing with money is one of my biggest challenges. From the outside, one would probably observe that my "fiscal house" is very much in order. And that would be true: we have no debt other than a reasonable mortgage; we spend within the means of our modest single-earner income; and we have a healthy amount of retirement investments and rainy-day savings proportional to our lifestyle. On the other hand, I tend to have a scarcity mentality when it comes to money. I'm way too risk-averse and anxious about it, and I often have a hard time being generous to others and to myself. When it comes to money, I've by no means arrived at some Zen-like freedom or the detachment of Saints Francis or Clare. I'm still very much on a journey toward wholeness. As challenging as it is to have a healthy relationship with money, especially in American culture, I'm guessing that you're probably on some sort of journey with it too. I hope we can be traveling companions.

## A BRIEF HISTORY OF MONEY

Before we dive into spirituality and simplicity when it comes to our dealings with money, it may be helpful to step back a bit and remind ourselves of what money actually is and where it comes from. It's a human invention, intended to serve a certain function; as the econ textbooks put it, it's a means of exchange and a store of value. But as we all know, it's become so much more than that. It's come to dominate just about every aspect of modern life, and while it can serve many useful purposes, it also has a shadow side that we would be foolish to ignore.

Before there was money, there was barter, whether between individuals or, more likely, between tribes. To take a much-too-simple example, maybe I'm good at growing apples but bad at raising chickens—and you're a great chicken farmer but a hopeless orchardist. In this case, we have what the economists call a perfect "coincidence of wants"—that is, you want what I can give, and vice versa. In that case, barter is easy. We just need to figure out the proper apple-chicken exchange ratio that makes us both happy. How many apples is a chicken worth?

Bartering is a beautiful, intimate way of exchanging value, but it has a lot of limitations. For one, what if the "coincidence of wants" breaks down? What if I'm good at growing apples, but I'd prefer smoked fish rather than chicken—and the fisherman doesn't like apples? All of a sudden, things get tricky, and we need to start doing complicated three-way and four-way and eight-way trades in order for everyone to get what they want, in the quantities they want, when they want it. And hence the invention of money: something that may not have value in and of itself, but we all agree to let it represent value. So if we agree that apples are worth so much money, and likewise chickens and smoked fish, then we can all receive money for what we produce and exchange that money for other things we need or want. Money solves the "coincidence of wants" problem, and it also solves the problem of my apples rotting before I can barter them all.

Likewise it solves the portability problem, because money is a lot easier to carry around than a bunch of apples or chickens—up to a point, at least. When you get enough of it, say in the form of gold coins, money also gets heavy and hard to manage, and it becomes a security risk. Eventually, societies that developed a money-based economy decided to store money with someone who could keep it safe, and so instead of carrying around coins, we just carried around the receipt indicating how many coins we had in storage. And then we discovered that instead of trading with actual coins, which are only marginally better than apples and chickens in terms of being heavy and bulky, we could trade with the paper receipts, trusting that they corresponded to the coinage we actually had in the bank.

All this seems sensible and straightforward enough, but from here it gets complicated and fuzzy, at least for me. In 1973, Americans went off the gold standard, meaning that the paper receipts we carried around—calling them dollars— no longer had to correspond to an equivalent amount of gold in a vault somewhere. We just basically agreed that paper money would itself be a stand-in for the value of the goods or labor we exchanged. Over the last several decades, dollars morphed into the bits and bytes of computer data, and money became almost completely abstract: a transaction between you and me just ends up as numbers in my account changing relative to yours. We also gave our federal governments the power to create money at will, out of thin air, by loaning money into existence through the central bank (known as the Federal Reserve in the U.S.), simply by printing paper dollars or typing new numbers into the Fed's computer system. The only reason that money has any value today is that our government says it does, we all have agreed, and we all trust our government to regulate its creation and use.

This brief history of money is woefully simplified and incomplete, but the main point is that money has always been a human invention to facilitate trade and to store value more conveniently and safely. In and of itself, money doesn't have any value at all. It only has the value that we agree upon. In that sense, money is a just a story we all agree to believe in: a common social agreement that depends entirely on trusting one another and our government. Money has also gotten more disconnected from the actual goods and services it represents and from the relationships between buyers and sellers. Once upon a time, the apple grower and the chicken farmer knew each other directly. But now, if you have money, those relationships can be indirect and anonymous. For money to serve us well, we have to create and make room for ways that money can connect us to one another with intentionality.

Another important point about our current money system is that because money is now created by central banks as interest-bearing debt, covering that interest means we need to create extra goods or services. We've created our own rat race: a system that requires constant economic growth. In other words, we need to keep monetizing or commodifying more of our world's resources and our human labor in order to keep the money system functioning. On a planet with finite people and resources, that's simply not possible for the long term.

## MONEY VERSUS WEALTH

There is a big and important difference between money and wealth. We may believe that wealth is just money in sufficient or abundant quantity, but I think this understanding is much too narrow. As I see it, wealth is much broader than mere money. Wealth is the sum total of what makes a rich and whole life for individuals and communities. Wealth comprises individual well-being, the quality of our relationships, the robustness of civic life and the social fabric, the health of local and global ecosystems, and at the broadest and deepest level for those of us who are religious, the spiritual connection we experience with God, with one another, and with our beautiful home planet.

As various indigenous peoples have shown us, it is possible to have great wealth while having little or no money. And I think we all know that the most important things in life can't be bought or sold. So money isn't the same thing as wealth—but there can be a relationship between them. In fact, there *should* be a relationship between money and true wealth. That's where the practice of simplicity comes in. How can we strip back all of the complex layers of meaning, value, power, and status that money has come to represent so we have room to use and relate to money in new ways, ways that serve true wealth and foster full flourishing for ourselves, for others, and for the planet?

## WEALTH WITHOUT MONEY: THE GIFT ECONOMY

The best way to get a healthy perspective on using money well is to start by talking about *not* using it. "Give to the emperor the things that are the emperor's," Jesus tells his disciples in Mark 12:17, "and to God the things that are God's." The way I interpret this passage, Jesus is saying there should be clear demarcations around the use of money. Money—the economy of government—has its useful and necessary place, but it shouldn't permeate every nook and cranny of our lives. Wendell Berry makes a distinction between the "little economy" of the human-created money system and the "Great Economy," which encompasses all the workings of the Earth ecosystem God created and sustains. The Great Economy runs not on money, but on gift: the gift of sunlight that makes all life possible, the gift of our benign and breathable atmosphere, the gift of liquid water, the complex web of reciprocal gift relationships that maintain the balanced beauty of the Earth's ecosystems. So one of the first steps in simplifying our relationship with money is to create spaces in our life where gift, not money, is the operative currency.

Most of the truly meaningful and satisfying activities in our lives have little to do with earning or spending money. Prayer and meditation, family time, hiking and walking, gardening, reading, writing, singing—these simple practices operate largely outside of the money economy and are deep sources of pleasure—or if not pleasure, at least satisfaction. Earlier this year, the pump on our septic system started malfunctioning. Convinced I could repair it myself, I climbed eight feet down into the sewage effluent tank to work on it, with my son keeping a leaf blower pointed at my head to supply me with enough fresh air so I wouldn't pass out from the methane. At one (very low) point in the process of multiple descents into this stinking abyss, the pipe I was working on burst under pressure, and I was doused with about a hundred gallons of raw sewage. Right about then, were I not so cheap and stubborn, would have been a good time to hire someone else to do my dirty work. But then I would have had to give up some great gifts: the satisfaction and empowerment I felt after finally completing that challenging and unpleasant repair, and the memories and stories that my son and I share about that adventure, laughing about it these many months (and many showers) later.

Cyndi and I have experienced something similar in the commitment we made to have at least one of us home with our children. At least until the COVID-19 pandemic forced it upon so many families, such a choice has become increasingly countercultural, even though not that long ago, there was no such thing as professional daycare. Our decision to keep our childcare out of the money economy has meant a lot less income for us, and it has often been quite a struggle for Cyndi, who has been the one staying at home with them, sacrificing for many years both the salary and the satisfactions of a professional career. And yet the gift she has given our kids has been one of the most inspiring things I have witnessed. Cyndi has built incredibly strong relationships with our children. She has nurtured and encouraged their unique talents and interests, and she has provided extra support for their struggles, especially in the years that they have been schooled at home. Even though the money economy ascribes no value to what she is doing, even though she has never earned a dime doing it and has, in fact, lost a great deal in opportunity costs, I know that in raising our three kids as she has, Cyndi has built an amazing amount of wealth, for our family and for the world. She has given the best of her time and her energy as a gift, and as is generally the way of real gifts, I believe it has been multiplied many times over.

## MONEY: NECESSARY EVIL OR QUALIFIED GOOD?

At this point, I've probably given the impression that I consider money at best a necessary evil, a fixture of a fallen world. And honestly, while I think that money can serve many useful purposes, I also think it can be a slippery slope to all kinds of trouble. Our current debt-based economic system is flawed in some pretty fundamental ways, given that it's predicated on the commodification of just about everything and has created massive, sinful degrees of inequality between individuals and nations. Capital may have helped us achieve many great advances, but it's also a big part of the way we exploit one another and exploit our world. Reflecting on an overhaul of our money system is well beyond the scope of this book, but I hope and pray that such changes do come about, and I think many of those changes will come from more of us making room for a "gift economy" that builds wealth separately from money.

Whatever my dreams of Eden, however, I recognize that we are far east of there now. With the human enterprise operating at such immense scale and with such complexity, it's impossible to live in the modern world and completely avoid dealing with money. So we will use money, at least some of the time. Living the value of simplicity in regard to money, then, means recognizing its power for good and its penchant for creating problems. We will constantly discern answers to two questions: When and how do we spend money? When is true wealth—for you and for the world—served by spending, and when is it served by not spending? I could easily make an argument that to have hired a local, sole proprietor septic repairman to fix our system would have helped him stay in business and would have saved me a lot of headache: a great use of money. For most people, that would have been the right choice. But for me, the wealth came in the form of bonding with my son and the feeling of empowerment from having solved a hard problem. There's no foolproof formula here, though I think it's always good to keep asking yourself if there are ways to address a particular need or want without money or with less of it, since in most cases that approach will involve more creativity, connection, cooperation with others, and generosity. But there are many instances in which the spending of money is exactly what can contribute to a better, more beautiful, and more truly wealthy world.

## SCARCITY, SUFFICIENCY, AND THE FLOW OF MONEY

Many of us think about money in terms of scarcity: the fear of losing it, of not having enough, and therefore the need to hold on to it tightly. Behind the veil of scarcity, though, there are more gracious ways to engage with money. What if we understood money as a form of energy that is meant to flow through our lives and through the world, rather than be hoarded and so become stagnant? To see money this way, to be willing to let it flow, requires letting go of fear and trusting instead that there is and will be enough for us and for others. Sufficiency—enoughness—is the middle way between scarcity and exploitative wealth. As Gandhi put it, the world has enough for everyone's need, but not enough for everyone's greed. Sufficiency is the way the birds of the air live, and the lilies of the field.

In our current economy, sufficiency is more the exception than the rule: we have many desperately poor people and nations alongside extremely rich people and rich nations. People who are rich, who have disproportionate control over our money system, have generally used their advantage to get richer, and this almost always happens at the expense of people who are poor. I take great encouragement from people who are trying to change that dynamic, like Nobel laureate Muhammad Yunus, the Bangladeshi economist and social entrepreneur who founded the Grameen Bank. Yunus envisions a world without poverty, without unemployment, and without harm to the Earth, and he insists that the proper use of money is the way to get us there. His method involves getting capital to flow toward the desperately poor through small-scale, favorable-term loans, which help them start small businesses that add valuable goods and services to their local communities. They may not get rich, but this flow of capital, through the practice of microfinance, gives them a chance to earn, save, and spend money so they can have sufficient food, shelter, education, healthcare, and other basic goods.

Earning money through work deserves its own chapter, so for the remainder of this chapter, let's just assume you have some capital at your disposal. What might simplicity look like in the saving, sharing, and spending of money?

## SAVING

Any capable financial planner will give you a couple of basic categories for your savings. You should build up your cash reserves for anticipated large expenditures, such as buying a house, replacing a furnace or car, taking a vacation, or sending the kids to college. You should also have a "rainy day fund" for unanticipated expenditures, such as a lost job, a car repair, a health challenge—usually equivalent to six months of your normal expenses. And you should, of course, save for your retirement. There is plenty of reliable guidance out there as to how much to save for retirement, based on your age, your current income, when you plan to retire, your desired lifestyle in retirement, and so forth. The problem is that although these amounts can be figured out in theory, it can be very hard to pin them down in practice. For my part, I find it very easy to imagine that in an uncertain world such as ours, my expenses—anticipated or not—will easily swamp my savings. What if I'm unemployed not for six months, but for a year? What if the kids don't go to a state school, but to an expensive private college? What if…? As a result of all these what-ifs, my answer to "how much to save?" often tends to be "everything I possibly can." It's a dangerous world out there, so goes my logic, and I can't count on (nor would I want) anyone to bail me out of a jam, so I'd better have a war chest that prepares me for anything.

There are all kinds of problems with that hoarding approach, however—even setting aside what it says about my lack of faith in the One who makes and sustains all of creation. If you've spent much time around a miser, you know that such a way of living just isn't much fun. Misers are so busy worrying about (or at least preparing for) the future that they have a very hard time embracing the present moment. There's something to be said for the discipline of delayed gratification, but in many cases, experiences delayed end up being experiences denied. In my case, as our kids get closer to leaving the nest, Cyndi and I want to make all the memories we can with them—and often that requires spending money we might otherwise have been tempted to save.

I think the only way to deal well with money is—wait for it—a family budget. I can hear you sighing as I write this, and

I'm sighing, too, because I've rarely been great about making or following a budget. But what I'm realizing about budgets is that they are not just about *limiting* your spending. They're also about *permitting* it. With a budget, I can make sure I have allotted enough to cover ongoing expenses and to save for anticipated and unanticipated outlays, but I can also build in money for the fun stuff: leisure, recreation, gifts, charitable giving. The times I have felt best about spending money are the times when I knew it was in the budget and there for the spending. It's definitely a discipline, but like most disciplines, it ends up providing more freedom with money, not less.

As I think about saving, I realize that while saving is a responsibility and a discipline, it's also a privilege. Whatever formulas the financial planners come up with in terms of responsible amounts to save, the underlying assuming is that you're going to have money *to* save—that is, that you can get your spending to come in under your current income. But plenty of people, through no personal failure, simply don't make enough money to cover basic expenses, much less to build a nest egg. Whether it's immigrant workers earning substandard wages (and remitting much of it back home), or blue-collar workers suffering layoffs, or gig workers who can't find steady and well-paying employment, plenty of people just are not keeping their heads above water. And because of historical inequities and intergenerational wealth transfer, the net worth of a typical white family tends to be ten times that of the typical Black family. What are the ethics of saving in the face of these facts, especially if, like me, you're a relatively privileged white person? What is the truly responsible thing to do—tend to your own needs or sacrifice some of your own savings to help others?

I'd like to put a pin in that thorny question and circle back to it shortly. For now, I'm going to assume that you're with me in regard to the need to save *something* for the future, even if the exact percentages and amounts require discernment. The question we then have to figure out is what to do with that money. What kinds of investments line up with the values of simplicity we've been talking about in this book?

This question is basically impossible to avoid. In an inflationary economy like ours, savings that don't earn a return greater than inflation are losing value. While it's good practice to have some cash that is earning little or no interest but is readily available for emergencies, most of our long-term savings needs to earn a decent return if it's going to have any purchasing power down the road. Again, a financial planner will help you figure out your tolerance for risk versus your appetite for return, as well as how often and how much you want to engage with your investments.

Beyond the questions of risk versus return or active versus passive investment management, I'll admit that I often ask myself about the ethics of *any* sort of investment, especially in light of the excesses of Wall Street. Investing is essentially using the money I have in order to make more, rather than earning money through labor that provides a good or a service. In my opinion, "money making money" is generally how the rich get richer while leaving the poor farther and farther behind. "Money making money" is so abstract that it becomes very easy to exploit both human labor and the rest of the natural world, which are the primary sources of value—especially when the rates of return we expect are generally higher than the rate of growth in most natural systems, meaning that we will tend to overharvest. But remembering Muhammad Yunus's heroic and creative work to provide much-needed capital for the very poor, I do think there are ways to invest that both deliver a reasonable return and help bring about a more just, more loving, more interdependent, more beautiful world.

For those who are inclined toward active engagement with their finances, there are plenty of new and creative opportunities to have your money flow toward things that serve the greater good. From the local to the global, from international community development organizations like Grameen Bank to your local credit union, it's possible to put your money to work providing loans (often collateral-free) to underprivileged people, unleashing their entrepreneurial efforts, helping them into home ownership, and so forth. I'm less knowledgeable here because I've not taken this plunge myself, but this kind of investing does resonate with me—especially the kinds of peer-to-peer arrangements where it's possible for the borrower and the lender to have a more direct relationship with each other. Anything that can remove layers of abstraction is a step that serves the values of simplicity and helps us toward a more connected, more humane world.

For those who haven't taken or don't wish to take the plunge into such radical forms of investment, a rapidly growing opportunity is "socially responsible investing" (SRI). In this form of investing, generally done through a mutual fund or an exchange-traded fund, you choose to invest in companies whose values you support—usually because of their leadership diversity, labor policies, and positive environmental record—and to avoid investments in companies that you don't want to support, such as those that produce fossil fuels, weapons, tobacco or alcohol, pornography, and so forth. More of these funds, which are backed by good research about the companies they invest in, are available now, and in general, their returns and management fees are reasonably comparable to non-SRI funds. I don't think this is a completely perfect solution for investing—or that it gets me off the hook in terms of continual discernment around investments—but having done socially conscious investing for over twenty years now, I feel it's a way to grow a retirement nest egg that is more in line with my core values.

## SHARING

When it comes to sharing your wealth, I don't have a specific formula to recommend. Even a "simple" answer about sharing, the 10 percent biblical tithe, isn't really so simple. Is it 10 percent of your gross income, or your net after taxes? Is it just 10 percent of the income you earn at your job, or 10 percent of your investment income too? Is 10 percent always the right figure, anyway? And how do you determine how much you might give to your house of worship versus other causes you want to support? What about your aging parents or your struggling children? What about the homeless man on the corner? Formulas can be helpful, but they often fail to address the complexity of our actual, specific situations.

Back when I was a cash-strapped graduate student, I sold my vehicle and gave all the money to my church, Holy

Comforter—the one time in my life when I had done anything comparable to Jesus's story of widow's mite. I did it because I had been moved from the heart. I had not yet referred to abstract ethical principles when I wrote that check. Instead, I was responding to a community I loved and whose needs I knew intimately. I wanted to give the gift I could give, because I knew it would make a difference in the church's very lean budget. It may have been irresponsible, but I've never regretted it. So while it's good to stand on principles and to make sharing a baseline practice in one's financial life regardless of how one happens to be feeling, I do think we're most inclined to share when we have a heart-level connection to a need—when we have a genuine desire to help, rather than a sense of duty or obligation.

As with many other times when wisdom comes from the mouth of babes, I've ended up learning this from my kids more than anyone else. Several years ago, our daughters asked for money around Christmastime, but not for themselves—they wanted to give it away. They were very concerned about people in other countries who didn't have enough to eat, so we helped them find organizations that were effective at addressing hunger issues. They cared deeply about animals, so they were thrilled when they could "adopt" various endangered creatures through the World Wildlife Fund. Helping them figure out how to spend that money was a lot of fun for all of us, and it felt good. I continue to learn from their generosity. They are, quite literally, willing to give away every last dollar they have, as a gift or a donation, because they get such pleasure in doing so. God loves a cheerful giver.

When it comes to sharing, what's most important isn't figuring out the exact right formula. What's crucial is to make room in your heart so you can be moved by the needs of others and can respond in the spirit of the gift. Sometimes that may look like a wildly generous donation. Other times, it may mean providing steady financial support to a family member. The point is the caring: recognizing that in the Great Economy, we swim in an ocean of generosity, and it's far easier to swim in it with open hands than with tight fists.

## SPENDING

Although we will delve back into this later, I do want to close this chapter with a few words about spending money, since that's the primary use of money. To return to one of the main themes of this book, when it comes to spending money, pleasure may actually be the best guide. To spend money well is to direct energy toward that which brings you the deepest satisfaction—not just what scratches an itch, fills a void, or provides a cheap thrill, but something that helps support something or someone you love and helps you become the person you want to be and bring about the kind of world in which you want to live. As I look back on my life thus far, the money I felt best about spending was for simple things: good food, experiences with Cyndi and our kids, good tools, good books, materials and supplies for making a home or farm or garden, and gifts. I felt best when I *believed* in what I was buying: that it was made well, that it would last, that it supported a craftsman or a community, that the spending of that money somehow made the world better rather than worse. In a world awash with so much substandard stuff, produced through the exploitation of people and planet, it's not easy to feel good about spending money. But when you can make purchases that line up with your values and support a more beautiful world, letting money flow in that way can be a great gift to yourself and to the world.

# six

# WORK

S ome sort of work is inevitable for pretty much all of us. And that is a good thing. Burdensome, sweat-of-the-brow toil may have come later in human history, but even the Garden of Eden (however historically or metaphorically you may understand that garden) required tending. Even our hunter-gatherer ancestors had to, well, hunt and gather. Jesus, the hardworking carpenter, took labor seriously. So did Paul, who was proud to be able to support himself through his trade as a tentmaker. St. Benedict wrote in chapter forty-eight of his *Rule* that "there should be specified periods for manual labor as well as for prayerful reading" and that "when they live by the labor of their hands, as our fathers and the apostles did, then they are really monks." Even St. Francis, the humble beggar, heard his call from God as a call to manual labor: to repair the crumbling church of San Damiano and two other small churches in the Umbrian countryside. Far from being a punishment for transgression, work is an essential part of the human vocation, part of what it means to be incarnated with material needs in a material world. Our calling is to find ways to work that align with the person we want to be and the world we want to see.

This isn't easy, of course. Many of us, much of the time, may feel trapped in meaningless, boring, dead-end jobs, chained to the hamster wheel or fighting our way up the corporate ladder because we're terrified that if we don't, we'll get knocked off that ladder and kicked to the curb. Or maybe we're not miserable at our jobs, but we're not inspired either. Maybe we're unemployed, fighting off depression and damaged self-esteem. Maybe we're retired, wondering what our work life meant and who we will be without it.

It's certainly true that simplicity means reducing the stranglehold that paid work has on our life, so there's plenty of room for other goods. But I don't think the endgame of simplicity is simply to minimize the role that work plays in our lives—for example, by retiring early, working minimal hours, or doing work that doesn't tax your physical or mental abilities. All of these seem to frame work as a necessary evil. I think the opposite is true: work is a necessary good that we should embrace as a fundamental path for human fulfillment. Work done well can be a wonderful means to good ends.

Before diving into what good work can look like and how it might serve the calling of simplicity, I want to be very clear about what I mean when I am talking about work. Certainly work can and does include what way we make our living— how we exchange our labor for money—and that's a primary focus of this chapter. But I understand work to be much broader than this. Seen in the most expansive way, work is how we participate in the Great Economy I mentioned in the previous chapter: the entire functioning of our world as a beautiful, interconnected ecological system, created and sustained by God. If that's what work means, then it's fair to say that animals work, as they participate in the ever-turning wheel of prey and predation. Trees work, as they play their patient, crucial roles in forest ecosystems. And when it comes to the realm of human work, our work certainly includes the job by which we earn money, but it also includes our child rearing (or grandchild rearing), our meal making, our dishwashing, our laundry folding, and our loose doorknob fixing. It includes our ushering at church, our volunteering on a nonprofit board or for the PTA, our caretaking for parents or for a wayward or disabled sibling, our gardening and lawn mowing. Work is the way we engage the world around us, for good and for ill.

When we see work in this broad sense, it becomes clear that most of us are called to work throughout our life in some capacity, regardless of compensation. The form of that work will differ according to our physical and mental abilities and will evolve according to our circumstances and our various life stages, but the call to work doesn't end when we start getting social security checks. My stepfather is a perfect example. He loved and believed in his paid work, providing financial planning advice for seniors, and he kept at it until he was almost eighty. But he finally did retire, and now he has given himself fully to his vocation of woodworking, kicking the cars out of the garage and outfitting it as a professional-grade woodshop. He's struck up some wonderful friendships with some fellow woodworkers in the neighborhood, and he and his buddies now spend countless hours in the shop together, turning out gorgeous bowls, cutting boards, and other handcrafts. For the most part, my stepdad gives all of his creations away, or if he does sell them, he donates the proceeds to local charities. Even late in his life, even after his professional career has ended, he is doing plenty of work—and loving every minute of it.

I hope I've dispelled any sort of notion that to lead a life shaped by the value of simplicity would minimize the role of work, in all of its various forms. If simplicity is about cultivating the freedom to choose that which honors the full flourishing of ourselves, our communities, and creation, then work, as one of our primary ways of engaging the world, is one of the main realms of activity in which that freedom gets worked out. Work, done rightly, is actually a path of simplicity. Done rightly, it is part and parcel of the spiritual life.

The key words, however, are *done rightly*. There are plenty of ways to work badly, to work in a way that harms yourself, others, and the broader world. So what might it mean to do work rightly? First, work done well can be a path for you to become your best self in the development of your particular gifts and talents and character. Second, good work is communal. It invites you into full participation with our interconnected, interdependent existence, so you can unite your efforts with those of others in a common task. Finally, good work is useful. It provides the goods and services that make for a flourishing life, for you and for others and for the other-than-human world. I'd like to unpack each of those a bit and see what each looks like in practice and in connection with the value of simplicity.

## BECOMING YOUR BEST SELF

Along with marriage and parenting, I would say that work is one of the main crucibles that has shaped the person I've become as an adult. The work I've done has called forth talents I didn't know I had and has demanded that I develop and strengthen them. I've had to learn financial management, human resource management, strategic planning, marketing, emotional intelligence, and a huge range of other things that keep the organizational wheels turning.

It's not just the skills we learn and hone, however. It's the person we become in the process of this learning by doing. Continually opening myself to the constant challenges of work, like the challenges of marriage, has forced me to confront my sins and shortcomings, has sanded off many rough edges, and has helped me learn both toughness and gentleness by turns. In fact, like most of the important aspects of the path of simplicity, it's been more about subtraction than addition. It's not been about accreting victories, promotions, and accolades, but rather, as the poet Rainer Maria Rilke once put it, growing by "being defeated, decisively, by greater and greater beings." This subtraction-rather-than-addition dynamic is important because good work ultimately is not about us, but about the world we serve through the goods or services we provide. Seen in this way, good work provides a built-in practice of humility, not only because we have to face failure so often, but also because such work will always be larger than we are. Work done well is a constant invitation to get over ourselves—both our successes and our failures—in service to a greater good. I know, for example, that the mission of the nonprofit I run is larger and more important than my particular role in the organization, however significant or small that role may be, and however well or badly I perform the role. When work is less about ego aggrandizement and more about serving a greater good, then whether we're paid or not, work becomes a gift: an opportunity to participate fully in the free-flowing generosity of the Great Economy. Work can be a realm in which you give your talents, your time, and your energy in order to serve others, whether that is bagging groceries, designing a building, or, as Cyndi does so faithfully in our household, lovingly preparing healthy meals. In that kind of creative generosity, we can become, as the saying goes, "the best version of ourselves."

## WORKING TOGETHER

Work, however, is not just about you, your character, and your ego, because pretty much all work is basically communal. Other than the lone hermit foraging for his own subsistence, most human endeavor involves working with and for other people. Even the self-employed entrepreneur is working for her customers. And most of us work as part of a team, whether it's a team of coworkers or family members. It's in the community that forms around common tasks that "real work" gets done: the project at hand, certainly, but also the work of relationships, which can be both a great blessing and a tremendous trial.

In an important sense, the communal aspect of work gets at part of the core essence of being human. First, like all creatures, we are made for interdependence. In every aspect of our lives, we do not and cannot exist apart from one another. What's more, we humans have developed an ability for social cooperation—not unlike trees in a forest ecosystem—that has enabled us to occupy almost every geography and climate on this planet. We are at our best and most truly human when we find ways to work together for a common good because that is what we've been created to do. It's in our very God-given nature.

To bring the values of simplicity to our work is to make room for the relationships that form in and around our work because it is these relationships that most fundamentally form and shape us. In my paid employment, I've been fortunate to have had a variety of colleagues. Some were fine role models and mentors who inspired and encouraged me. Some have annoyed me into learning patience, acceptance, and strong boundaries. Many have been good, kind, and competent—a pleasure and privilege to work with. Some I've had to let go of, whether on good terms or bad. All of these relationships have given me the chance to grow and learn. Sometimes I've embraced the opportunity and become the better for it. Sometimes I've just brooded and complained, mostly to my infinitely patient wife. But good or bad, all of these relationships have formed and shaped me, as all relationships should. In fact, I think it's fair to say that this work of relationships has been just as much effort as the actual doing of the tasks. And that's a good thing. In the end, what's more important for us as members of a common human family—what we accomplish in our work or the relationships we've built and the community we've fostered in the doing of it?

## SUPPORTING A FLOURISHING WORLD

Finally, good work provides the goods and services that are necessary for a flourishing world. If work as individual fulfillment and communal enterprise are about means, here I'm getting at the question of ends: What sorts of things should work create? I don't believe it's wise to produce anything we might dream up, at the greatest possible scale, merely to pump up the gross domestic product. That seems to be the approach we've taken in America, somehow conflating the production of goods and services with happiness and contentment, under the assumption that if the GDP grows, so does our individual and collective well-being. But beyond a certain minimum level of production that meets everyone's basic physical needs, there's no strong correlation between a growing economy and our well-being as individuals or communities, much less a flourishing Great Economy.

If we want to work well, we'll try to create only the things that truly add value to human life and to the good of creation; in amounts that are sufficient but not excessive, wasteful, or harmful; in a way that is honorable and just. How else can we truly believe in the work we do? Fortunately, there are many opportunities to do work that we can deeply believe in, whether it's through the arts, science, business, or any other ways we can pursue beauty, knowledge, fairness, and health. My dream is that we find ways for more people to find ways to earn their livelihood through work that contributes to the healing of the world, rather than its destruction. Wouldn't that be a great rewriting of the story of money and economy?

Much of the work we do has some thread of ambiguity woven into it, however. Plenty of jobs not only fail to add any real value to the world, but actually degrade workers, customers, or the health of creation. Plenty of people work at jobs they know full well are destructive to the social fabric and to more than the human world, but the rewards of income, status, or power are such that they are willing to sell out to them. In these kinds of situations, some public accountability is in order. We have to call a spade a spade and ask people in such positions to defend the utility of such work or, if they can't do that, to explain why they continue to choose it. For example, I don't think there is any justification for working in nuclear weapons development, or clear-cut timbering of old-growth forests, or exploitive and risky financial specu-lation, or policy work that enables such industries to thrive. The argument "I was just doing my job" simply isn't good enough—even if that job is bringing home the bacon for your family. We human beings have more agency than that. At some point you just have to choose the good, even when that means some sacrifice.

If you have a choice, that is. I know that what I just wrote may sound unsympathetic toward those who are trapped in work that is not good, so I want to acknowledge that many people really do face difficult, limited options for their live-lihood. I'm thinking, for instance, about Appalachian coal miners who are destroying their own lungs and landscapes because the economy in their region offers them—at least right now—no other alternatives to stay out of poverty. In situations like this, I would make a clear distinction between the work and the worker. Even if the work isn't good work, can't we at least honor the worker who is doing her best in a difficult situation? I certainly recognize the difficulty of being in such a dilemma where one has to choose between two evils. The harm that does to one's psyche is real and substantial. And can't we honor the skill and knowledge that workers may bring to such work—while trying like mad to find different, better ways to employ those gifts?

## WORK AS GIFT

The irony here is that while many jobs are unnecessary in the Great Economy and even harmful to it, plenty of good work goes unrewarded and even unrecognized by our current economic system. Certainly all the domestic arts, from raising fine children to raising fine vegetables, fall in this category. So do efforts to defend or repair the Earth's forests, prairies, waterways, and other crucial but threatened ecosystems. As a result, doing good work may mean doing some, much, or all of our work for little or no monetary compensation, but instead offering our work as a gift to others and to the world. Practically speaking, maybe that means dialing back our lifestyle so we can afford to work at a meaningful job even if the pay isn't great, or reducing the hours at our paying work so we have time to do other work that makes our heart sing. Those were the commitments Cyndi and I made early in our marriage; she wanted to be able to stay home with our kids for their early years, and I wanted to be able to do work I believed in even if it didn't pay that well, so we had to figure out how we could live on a modest household income. And for almost twenty years, we've found ways to do it. It has meant some creativity and sacrifice, but it has brought us many blessings.

As with most things related to simplicity, there are no cookie-cutter solutions here. What I'm most interested in helping you do is to ask questions of the work you do so you can discern—with the guidance of God's still small voice in your heart and the input of friends, family, and community members—the ways in which the work you do actively contributes to the good of the Great Economy and to your own flourishing. When you find that kind of resonance, then work—paid or unpaid, small-scale or world-scale—becomes divine vocation.

# seven

# PLAY

One of my favorite photos is one I happened to snap of our daughter Clare when she was about four years old. She was dressed up in her well-worn pink princess dress, running wild and barefoot through one of our hayfields, innocent, overjoyed, without a care in the world. I have returned many, many times to that picture. It not only brings back a beautiful chapter of our parenting, but it's a great reminder of what it can look like to be fully and truly alive. As parents, Cyndi and I (mostly Cyndi) have tried very hard to create the space where such moments can happen, to encourage and protect in our children the playful spark that is their birthright.

Play was a lifeline for Cyndi and me through difficult periods of our own childhoods. She spent countless hours of make-believe and high-brow tea parties with her sisters, gathering in secret, sacred places around her family's hillside Pennsylvania farm. I camped, hiked, biked, canoed, motorcycled, and off-roaded my way through the awkward transitions of adolescence and the pain of my parents' divorce. We both gravitated toward making music, through singing and various instruments. Somehow, we both knew that play was essential medicine.

## THE IMPORTANCE OF PLAY

As often happens, scientific research has confirmed human instinct and common sense about the importance of play. Rough-and-tumble play helps children improve coordination, proprioception, and other vital elements of physical development. But according to psychiatrist Stuart Brown and others, play also helps us learn fairness, inclusion, and other positive social attitudes and behaviors. In fact, Brown's research into serial killers and other violent offenders found an important common link in their backgrounds: the radical suppression of free play in their formative years. Play makes us more cognitively flexible, imaginative, and creative. It may seem purposeless, but it serves a larger, absolutely essential role in helping us to become fully human, such that child development expert Maria Montessori built an entire system of education predicated on the importance of play. What's more, science is teaching us that play isn't something human beings should grow out of. Play looks different for adults than it does for children, but it is as crucial for us as grown-ups as it was for us as kids.

## CHILDREN AT PLAY

"Play," wrote Maria Montessori, "is the work of the child." To the extent that I've learned to play as an adult—and I am still very much a beginner at this—our children have been my greatest teachers. They are the best play-ers I've ever met. We didn't pull off some parenting miracle for that to happen. We tried to give them a mostly analog childhood, making sure they had simple, sturdy, usually nonelectronic toys. Many days we pushed them out the door and just let them make up their own fun—which they managed to do with sticks, rocks, dirt, cardboard boxes, and anything else they found at hand. Cyndi read to them in the evening and—miracle of miracles—still does, even though they are now all teenagers. Perhaps most importantly, we have generally allowed them to be bored so they would have to use their own imaginations and make their own games. And I still marvel at the results: even as they are becoming wise and grown up beyond their years, they have somehow retained the magic of childhood. All three of them still spend hours out in the woods or in the yard, creating entire make-believe worlds. Eva and Clare are voracious fiction readers, vacuuming up J.R.R. Tolkien, Ursula Le Guin, and Rosemary Sutcliff among others. They've also become writers, filling dozens of composition books with stories about various imaginary lands and peoples. Eli spends hours building with Legos, playing with model trains, and engaging in other activities I feared he would outgrow long ago. Somehow, they have retained their birthright of play-fulness. And by whatever miracle—and well beyond my deserving—they have continued to want me to be part of their play, part of their lives. That invitation, to recover the blessings of play even in my middle years, is the one of greatest gifts I've ever been given. More than almost anything else in my life, it has made God's grace real to me.

## PLAYING AS AN ADULT

Fortunately, there are plenty of ways to make room for play even alongside grown-up cares and responsibilities. If even I can do it, despite taking myself and the world much too seriously, then anyone can.

Much of adult playfulness has to do with attitude. It's possible to bring a playful spirit into almost anything we do, even into all of our chores and responsibilities. It starts with giving yourself permission to be playful and reminding yourself that play is essential, not frivolous. It also entails creating space around your tasks that isn't loaded with strict expectations of how something is supposed to go. When you demand that an activity unfold in a certain way and on a certain time frame, you'll drain any playfulness right out of it, with misery and frustration usually taking its place. I learn that again and again with household projects, which invariably don't go according to plan or schedule. When that happens, you have a choice: fight against reality and lose or find the humor in the situation and allow your agenda to flow in accord with the facts on the ground. Plenty of times, when fixing cars or tractors, I'd invariably encounter a stuck bolt. When I was in non-playful, type-A mode, I would curse the bolt and the gods, and invariably I'd end up with skinned knuckles and a more serious repair. But when I could take a breath, perhaps even laugh a bit, and create a bit of spaciousness around the situation, it always went better—and was a lot more fun. Curiosity helps too. When you move wide-eyed through the world, wondering what will come next and willing to be surprised, you will hold things more lightly. I have a few scientist friends who exemplify this kind of adult playfulness. They are endlessly fascinated by the world, and when they're out in the field doing research, they're just like big kids.

While you can bring playfulness into anything you do, it's helpful to have activities that are purely and simply play. For me, a favorite way to play has been rock climbing. I love being outside and connecting with the landscape. I love the adrenaline rush and the elements of controlled risk. I love the camaraderie that climbing requires, since you always have to have a partner on the other end of the rope. I love the physical and mental challenges involved. When you are clinging to a cliff face by your fingertips, trying to find your next moves, it tends to focus the mind. I've been meditating for almost thirty years, and my mind still wanders plenty when I'm on my cushion. But when I'm on a crag, life becomes very, very simple, and I have a clarity of attention that I rarely experience in any other circumstances. Adult play certainly doesn't have to be as intense as rock climbing, though. A good book, a leisurely stroll, a dedication to an instrument, an art, or a craft—so many things can make our heart sing without having to accomplish anything tangible.

## MAKING ROOM FOR PLAY

What gets in the way of play, and how can simplicity help us stay playful throughout our lives? For those of us who are religious, I'm afraid that religion has often been unhelpful in this regard. Whether it's suspicion of the body and its pleasures, overzealous moral scrupulosity in its various forms, extreme piety, or even radical, religiously inspired commitments to justice, a lot of religious people end up not being very playful. And why would they be? After all, Christians follow a Savior who was crucified and look to saints who were often extreme ascetics, martyrs, or both. Upon concluding a rosary, we Catholics "send up our sighs, mourning and weeping in this valley of tears." Where's the fun in any of this?

Despite all this, I still think that religious faith can invite us into play. The Dalai Lama, who carries the grief and hardships of so many exiled Tibetan people, still calls himself a "professional laugher." And the venerable St. Teresa of Avila, no stranger to tough times, prayed with good humor that the Lord deliver us from "sour-faced saints." I'd like to think that the first chapters of Genesis describe a playful God who brought about the world in a burst of playful creativity. Likewise, I like to imagine Jesus, serious as he was about his ministry, as having a wicked sense of humor, willing to attend parties, to tell stories, and to turn regular conventions on their head. And if you really want to get down to it, prayer itself can be a form of play, especially in its quiet, contemplative forms when you're basically just sitting around doing nothing. That may sound disrespectful, but if you start expecting things out of your prayer time, or of God, your religiosity becomes far more about you than about God and creation. I find it a wonderful, delicious irony that, as Jesuit priest James Martin has pointed out, the mystical masters from various contemplative traditions actually ended up having a very playful side. Perhaps my favorite is the Sufi poet Hafiz, who thought that if you were a religious seeker and wanted to be wise, it was best to "cast all your votes for dancing." Perhaps (and I hope so!) this is what a truly simple spiritual life looks like, after we begin to cling less tightly to our attachments: a really good, playful sense of humor.

One of the best ways to ruin play is to turn your recreation into an achievement-oriented performance. When I go rock climbing, I often fall into the trap of thinking I should be climbing harder and harder routes. While challenging yourself can be a good thing, it can also, unfortunately, be a very effective way to ruin the fun. One of my climbing partners is still going strong at age seventy, and I try to follow his advice: the best climber isn't the one who crushes the hardest grades but the one who has the most fun, even if that's on easier routes. Having goals and pushing yourself can be a form of enjoyment, but only if you can maintain a degree of detachment and humility that allows you to love your activity for its own sake, rather than because it bolsters your ego. In that respect, playing well is like praying well, since both can bear similar fruit.

In many forms of play, it's tempting to think you have to purchase the latest, greatest equipment and accessories for your pursuit. Just a few weeks ago, in a bike store, I drooled over a fancy mountain bike that would have set me back almost three times as much as my first vehicle. And I would still have to pedal it! In play as in so many other areas, simplicity asks us to ask ourselves: How much is enough? Do I need the fancy heart rate monitor, the latest moisture-wicking fabric, the lightest carbon-Kevlar bike frame? Or can I still have fun without having to break the bank? Because if you are going to play that hard, of course you're going to have to work hard to afford those kinds of toys—and doesn't that defeat the point? So, as in all things simple, I feel a certain freedom in not needing the best gear. When we go mountain biking, my son often shakes his head at my rusty, thirty-year-old bike with its balky, mismatched components. But I can have plenty of fun on that old beater, and I'm a lot less worried about breaking or scratching it than I would be about the expensive Holy Grail bike that beckoned to me in the shop. Having decent equipment is nice, but there's a point of diminishing returns, and making room for play means finding that point amidst the siren calls of consumer culture.

Another obstacle to play is a version of the grass-is-greener argument: the idea that you have to go somewhere exotic in order to have fun. My mom and stepdad have always loved to travel, but age and health issues began to slow them down, and then the coronavirus pandemic put an absolute halt to any farther-flung journeys. I was nervous about what being stuck at home would do to them, but it's been a surprisingly good experience. They have radically changed their hectic pace and concentrated on at-home pursuits. My stepdad has his woodworking, Mom reads and knits and works on art projects, and together they burn through Great Courses DVDs like Oreo cookies. When they really began to go stir-crazy at home, they became—I'm laughing as I write this—Sunday drivers. Almost every Sunday afternoon, they take a meandering day trip in their Subaru wagon, exploring the nooks and crannies of small-town Indiana and Kentucky. In their latter years, they have realized that as fascinating as the wide world is, it's possible to have plenty of fun while staying close to home. That's more our speed too. I do love our occasional longer road trips to see extended family or, for us landlubbing Midwesterners, the ocean. But it's also nice to know that amidst those rarer trips, there's always a playful adventure awaiting close at hand.

## PLAYING WITHIN OUR MEANS

I think it's quite possible that in future decades, climate change or shortages of energy and resources may limit our ability to play in the way we do now. Hopefully we'll find ways to move ourselves around more efficiently—for example, high-speed trains or solar-powered airships instead of carbon-intensive jets, or electric cars rather than gas-hogs. But we may just have to travel less—which, let's face it, is the current situation of billions of people in this world. And we (or our planet) may not be able to afford all the fancy toys that are often part and parcel of our play. Many people can't afford them even now. The good news is that simplifying our play doesn't have to feel like deprivation. In fact, playing within our personal and planetary means can be a path to creativity, community, and connection—to our best selves and to the rest of the natural world. That's an adventure worth having, and it can start right at home.

# eight

# STUFF

'll start with the basic question: Why do most of us end up with so much stuff? I don't think it's because we're selfish, depraved monsters who shovel stuff into the gaping void where our soul used to be. In fact, I don't think there's a single, simplistic reason that has led to the need for a public storage rental industry. It's more like one thing added to another thing added to another, and the cumulative effect is daunting—in our own lives and in our culture.

One of the reasons, I believe, is some generic version of Moore's Law. Moore's Law was originally developed to describe the exponential increase in computing power relative to cost: the power of a computer doubles roughly every two years, while its cost halves. Given how the sleek, powerful, but not-that-expensive laptop I'm using to write this book compares to the old room-sized mainframe computers of yesteryear, or the fact that my cell phone has significantly more computing power than what brought astronauts to the moon and back, I take Moore's point. And though the specifics will vary, a similar phenomenon has taken hold with most manu-factured goods since the dawn of, well, manufacturing. A small-screened, boxy, black-and-white television would have set me back the equivalent about $8,500 in 1958. Today I can pick up a large, high-definition, flat-screen, smarter-than-I-am TV for just a few hundred dollars. The Industrial Revolution has inflicted tremendous harm to individual workers and communities (especially in the distant countries where most of our stuff is made) and to the Earth, but wow, we have to admit that it has delivered the goods. Unimaginable technological and manufacturing advances, coupled with an economy that doesn't factor in all the hidden and not-so-hidden costs of our stuff, have made it not only possible but relatively normal to fill our homes brimful of gear and gadgets without neces-sarily emptying our bank accounts. Ditto to cheap clothing, cheap furniture, and all the other not-so-high-tech-but-still-dirt-cheap goods (or not-so-goods) that are available to us for pennies on the dollar compared to a century ago. Set aside for the moment that many, if not most, of these goods are designed to fall apart and need replacing (not, heaven forbid, repairing) in short order—usually not long after the warranty has expired.

It's not just that stuff is cheaper to get, but it's also easier to get. Amazon and other online retailers were busy preparing the obituaries for a lot of local brick-and-mortar retail estab-lishments before the pandemic hit, and since then they've been pounding the last nails in the coffins. There's plenty to lament in that victory—though I have to be honest: I won't miss shopping malls one bit—but you can't deny how unbelievably easy it has become to have more and more stuff appear at your door. Between one-click ordering and one-day delivery, perusing Amazon's online wares has become a strenuous exercise in willpower and restraint, lest we fill our shopping cart with stuff we don't need and can't afford. Isn't there some app that helps you put the brakes on such impulses?

That we should need such high doses of willpower and restraint does lead me to ponder how much freedom we really have vis-à-vis the machinery of our consumerist economy. I think we tend to amass stuff not only because we can, but also on some level because we must; for most of us, the modern consumerist trend is a form of compulsion that is very hard to resist. Why?

On one hand, there's plenty of external pressure. An entire industry of advertising and marketing has grown up to force-feed us the habits of consumption. Before the days of DVRs, I remember how annoyed I would get at television commercials. Now, awash in targeted advertising that apparently knows every website I've ever visited, I look back on my complaints about TV ads and find it sadly ironic that I didn't have any idea what was coming. I'm sure I'm not the only one who has been creeped out by the algorithm-driven, relevant-content ads that follow us around the internet like dogs sniffing out the trail of our data exhaust. Everywhere we turn, someone is trying to sell us something. We now seem to live in a Total Marketing State, where Big Brother isn't the government, but rather the advertising industry, fueled and guided by Big Data. If I were stronger and more principled, I'd foreswear online shopping and be extremely careful about my online privacy. But that's my point: I've failed to do that, and you probably have too. Willpower is a finite resource, and I generally spend mine avoiding plenty of other temptations—and eating my spinach.

If there's anything more insidious than ubiquitous advertising, it's the guerrilla marketing campaign unwittingly waged against us by everyone around us, including our peers. Of course there's the tired old set piece of keeping up with the Joneses in a constantly escalating arms race over the best car, the fanciest TV, the hippest yoga pants, the biggest house. I'm sure we spiritually inclined people can easily see through that game, right? Honestly, I'm not so sure. We may be able to see through the most blatant forms, but there's something subtler than that, something that seems to be in the water we drink and the air we breathe: this sense of inevitability that *of course* we will replace our cell phone every two years because it's outdated, and our vacuum cleaner every three because it fell apart under normal use and is unrepairable. Consumption-on-steroids is the new normal.

We're not just puppets and pawns of the advertising industry or flailing helplessly and haplessly against the powerful current of cultural norms, though. Some of our consumption compulsions come from within. I don't think it's too strong to use the language of addiction—or at least, attachment—when it comes to how we relate to our stuff. Obviously, there's a spectrum here. Relatively few of us, thank goodness, are shopaholics perpetually on the brink of bankruptcy, but I would wager that almost all of us have made plenty of purchases because we were bored, restless, unhappy in our relationships, anxious, and affected by any number of other mental health challenges. The definition of addiction is trying to fulfill a need with something that won't ultimately fill that need, and then when it inevitably fails, doubling down on what's not working—and so the vicious cycle begins. But don't we want to find a way to own stuff without being owned by it? If not, then how in the world can we explain the Marie Kondo phenomenon?

## BECOMING A TRUE MATERIALIST

Throughout the planning and writing of this book, I've resisted the term *minimalism*. That's partly because I've read enough of minimalist literature to know that many who proudly claim the minimalist moniker are so unbelievably more hardcore than I am that I have no right to bandy that term about. But it's also because there's a thread running through that movement that seems to idealize having the absolute bare minimum of things, to the extent that many minimalists keep an accurate count of how many items they own. To my mind, such an approach can just be a new form of obsessing about one's stuff, and it also seems to imply the simplistic equation that stuff equals bad and less stuff equals good. Neither of those seem especially helpful to me.

It's true that stuff always has a cost. It costs us time, money, and psychic energy to acquire, move, store, maintain, use, and dispose of. Once, back on our farm, I tallied up how many gasoline engines I had to tend. It was sobering to run out of fingers on both hands well before I got to the end of the count. I've since whittled that number down considerably, but now it's battery-powered equipment. How many things do I have to plug in every night, or feed fresh batteries like candy to a hungry toddler? Cell phones, tablets, laptops, watches, smoke alarms, flashlights, kitchen scales, remotes, cordless drills—oh my. I simply don't want to know how much of my life-energy I have given to my stuff.

Stuff also has human and environmental costs, in the making of it and in the disposing of it. Those costs are largely hidden from us. They rarely show up in the price. We generally don't see close-up the huge, open-pit mines that supply many of the materials. We don't experience the factory conditions in which stuff is manufactured or live by the smokestacks and slurry ponds and effluent pipes. We don't see the mountains of improperly managed waste that our things become when their lifecycle is at an end.

There has to be some kind of middle ground in dealing with our stuff that doesn't demonize having things but also recognizes and takes seriously our stuff's various human and environmental costs. Again, no easy answers or formulas here, but to me, the best way to deal with stuff is to become truly materialist.

To become a true materialist doesn't mean going the route of many scientists or the New Atheists and assuming that all of reality is composed simply of physical material. That belief—and let's be clear, it's a belief just as much as religious faith is—certainly doesn't work for people who have spiritual commitments, but it increasingly doesn't even work within the scientific worldview either, as science discovers more mysterious forms of energy and relationship that simply defy understanding and control. No, to be a materialist simply means *to love and honor the material*. To be a materialist is to sink heart-deep into a faith that the world in its entirety is holy, created and sustained by a divine power both wonderful and ineffable. To be a materialist is, to use my Christian language, to believe fully in the Incarnation: that God so loved the world that God *became* the world, dwelling within it from the very beginning of creation, and that God delights in and sustains the cosmos at every moment.

When you begin to see the world in this way—in glimpses at first, then more deeply throughout a lifetime of spiritual practice—it's possible to make the leap from experiencing stuff as mere possessions, which implies zero-sum individual ownership and control, to experiencing stuff as sacramental. In the Catholic imagination, a sacrament is something perceivable to the senses—something material—that is at the same time a spiritual reality, opening a window into the presence of the divine. The Eucharist, for example, is bread and wine: fully material, fully the fruit of the earth and the work of human hands, but also shot through with spiritual significance. We know the official sacraments of the Church, but there's also a broader sense of the sacred. Thomas Merton, the Cistercian spiritual master, captured it well in this simple phrase: "Everything that is, is holy."

And what does it mean to be sacred—to be woven, warp and weft, of divine fabric? For one, it means that all the raw material of this world and all the human and other-than-human creatures of this world are divinely given gifts, deserving of reverence and respect for their place in the Great Economy, and therefore not simply expendable. To be sacred also means to participate fully—even if not consciously—in the ongoing dance of relationships, which are the fundamental divine reality, as good Trinitarian theology claims. To be sacred means that everything and everyone (human and non-human) can be a conduit and a container for beauty and meaning. Everything, if we just learn to see with the right eyes, is shining like the sun. And it means, in an important way, that ownership and possession are ultimately a fiction. We dance with "our" things for a short while, and then either before we die or afterward, they move on to a different partner.

## MAKING GOOD CHOICES

Such language soars into the abstract, but what can it tell us when we haul it down to earth and ask it for practical counsel about how to deal well with the daily stuff of our lives? I hope that to treat the things of Earth as sacred rather than as possessions means that, as much as possible, we relate to stuff with gratitude and appreciation, knowing that they are gifts. As I look around our house, I see so many things that carry profound meaning and story. On one wall hangs the sculpture I commissioned a local artist to create for Cyndi when she graduated with her master's in theological studies. Our kitchen table was handmade by my stepfather out of rock maple that I harvested from our old farm. Another local artist created gorgeous wall quilts that we gave as gifts to each of our daughters. I regularly use a hand-ground Finnish filleting knife that belonged to my grandfather. Out in the garage are the power tools I used to build our previous home and fill it with trim and cabinetry—which I hope to do again before I die. There are also simple old hand tools belonging to my other grandfather, including a stainless steel flat-blade screwdriver that he, a machinist, fabricated himself. In the barn is our faithful tractor, which has plowed fields and gardens, made hay, cleared driveways, hauled firewood, and done countless other chores. I'm sure you could tell similar stories about things in your own home. Yes, we have too much stuff, and a lot of it is simply junk, but I am deeply grateful for so much of it because so much of it also holds precious memories for us, reminding us of experiences we have had and people and places we love. I would never want to get rid of such stuff just for minimalism bragging rights or the abstract principle of having fewer things.

So if the goal is to mostly have things that we can feel deeply good about, in which we see the sacred shining through, how do we make conscious choices when we acquire things? I don't think it's realistic that all of our stuff has to "spark joy," to borrow Marie Kondo's famous phrase—I just can't get there when it comes to replacing the battery in my car's key fob. But I do think it's worthwhile to be discerning in our purchases. We can ask to what extent something is well-made and durable, and how easily it can be repaired, repurposed, or recycled (in that order). We generally have to pay a premium for high-quality stuff, but in most cases, I think it's worth it. In the realm of tools, for example, I've learned that there is no such thing as an inexpensive tool. There are high-quality, expensive tools that work well and last. There are cheap tools, but they end up being expensive, too, because they break and require replacing. As much as you can, go for the good stuff.

Beyond these basic questions are the important but far more difficult meta-questions that relate to the four main themes of

simplicity in this book. Does this thing bring me real pleasure and satisfaction? Does it serve my spiritual growth, or
at least is it not a hindrance? Does it support my sense of
solidarity with the poor? Does it reflect my desire to treat
the Earth with kindness? Answering the first two is hard to
do on the front end, because how can we really know ahead
of time what will bring us joy and serve our growth? But it's
possible to develop good instincts around this. Most of us
know that buying cheap, flimsy junk doesn't make our soul
sing. The latter two questions are also challenging to answer,
but with GoodGuide and similar apps, it's becoming easier
to figure out where our stuff came from, who made it, and at
what environmental cost. You can certainly spend all of your
time and energy researching your purchases, and it's easy to
become paralyzed. The main thing is to keep trying to buy
things that serve your own well-being and the good of the
Great Economy.

### LETTING GO

Finally, a few words about getting rid of things. If you're
reading this book, it's probably not because you've "arrived"
at a Zen-like state of simplicity and just need a pat on the
back and some encouragement to stay the course. I assume
that you struggle, like I do, to simplify your life, and I likewise
assume that you, like me, have too much stuff. So how do we
go about the necessary process of letting go?

It can be tempting to set rigid, perfectionist standards for
ourselves and invest plenty of energy in trying to pare our
belongings down to some absolute minimum, but this usually
ends in failure (or we become impossible to live with). So we

have to approach the process of letting go with humility and some degree of flexibility. When we moved most recently, we did a *lot* of aggressive purging, and I'd say 80 percent of that was necessary, felt good, and was the right approach. But we also gave away or threw out many things that we actually ended up needing and just had to purchase again. A bit more judiciousness and discernment might have been helpful, but in the fog of urgency that moving was for us, we did the best we could.

While a hard-and-fast rule and a take-no-prisoners approach probably aren't the best ideas, it makes sense to have some regular practice by which we look at our relationship with our things, asking if they are still contributing to the kind of life we want to live. Maybe on a monthly, seasonal, or annual basis, you consciously inventory your stuff and screw up the courage to get rid of some of it. This can be a joyful process, especially if you take the time to honor your stuff for its service in your life and perhaps even consider giving it to someone you know who could appreciate and use it well. I know that I got a special thrill in giving my treasured Swiss Army knife, which I'd had since boyhood, to my son. Perhaps one day he'll give that same knife to his son or daughter. I've also enjoyed fixing things simply to give them away so that they serve the next person well. Another trick we've tried is to get rid of one or even two items for every new item we acquire. I try to do that with clothing, and it has kept my wardrobe to a manageable scale. It can also help to have an accountability partner—usually your spouse—and agree to consult each other when considering a purchase over a certain amount.

One beautiful upshot to letting go of your things—and more broadly, letting go of the idea of possessions more generally—is that an exciting alternative arises: sharing. Though America tends to be more of an individualist, ownership culture—certainly as we defined ourselves against the collectivist communist regimes of China and the USSR—I can at least imagine scenarios in which it isn't necessary for every single person on the block to own and maintain their own weed eater or log splitter or even car. Back when we lived on the farm, I owned some farming equipment in common with another farmer, and both of us got the benefit of using it at only half the cost. As Zipcar, urban electric scooters, rent-a-bikes, and other experiments are proving out, you don't have to own something to use and enjoy it. Outside of monasteries, most of us will likely never get to the common-purse way of life described in the second chapter of the Acts of the Apostles, but there is plenty of beautiful middle ground between that ideal and to each his or her own.

## LETTING OUR STUFF SERVE US

As I'm sure is clear by now, I'm not trying to give you a particular formula for subtracting things from your life. My point is simply that we would do well to cultivate intentionality rather than undue attachment in our relationship with our belongings. Our things can fill our homes with stories and meaning—or they can just fill our homes. Knowing the difference is a matter of paying attention, so that instead of us serving our stuff, our stuff serves our own longing for deep satisfaction, spiritual maturity, and solidarity with others and our beloved, beautiful Earth.

# nine

# THE DIGITAL WORLD

Over the last few decades, the digital world has become ubiquitous in America and much of the globe. Few things make me feel my age more than realizing that I belong to the last of the analog generations. Unlike the millennials and younger folks in the generations after me, I've witnessed the rise of the personal computer, cell phones, the internet, email, smartphones, iPods, tablets, digital social media platforms, and content streaming services. Just the other day I was explaining to my teenage son about old data tape drives, floppy disks, and dial-up modems, and his look of incomprehension made me feel like an absolute fossil.

The accident of when I was born has given me the great gift of being able to remember what it was like when ones and zeroes, in all of their various forms, did not hold sway in almost every domain of our lives. This makes me a digital immigrant, compared to the digital natives in the generations following mine who are naturally habituated to the digital world because it's the only world they've ever known. I already hear myself starting to sound like an old geezer here, complaining about the young whippersnappers buried nose-deep in their phones, but I'm deeply grateful to have grown up straddling the line between analog and digital realms. I'd like to think that gives me some perspective.

## GIFTS AND TEMPTATIONS OF THE DIGITAL AGE

We can all appreciate much of what the brave new digital world has delivered to us. My smartphone has saved me countless wrong turns, wasted trips, and forgotten grocery items. It has let me use my commute time to catch up with family and friends. Netflix and Amazon streaming services have made for many special Friday pizza-and-movie nights for my family, and my son and I have bonded over several series we've streamed while exercising—even old *Star Trek* episodes and other dated shows in which I thought he'd have no interest. YouTube has been an absolute godsend for a handy, build-it-or-fix-it-yourself kind of person like me. Want to rebuild your lawnmower carburetor? There's a YouTube video for that. Lay bathroom tile? Check. Perform brain surgery? Probably. Where the heck was YouTube when I was building a house, for crying out loud? And don't get me started on podcasts and audiobooks. With a voracious appetite for information and a lot of time devoted to manual work, I was an early adopter of MP3 players, and I've probably listened my way through the equivalent of several graduate degrees by now.

The benefits the digital revolution has delivered us are legion, but so too are the challenges and pitfalls. In many ways, our digital technologies are not serving us well. Constantly checking or being pinged by email, texts, news alerts, and social media notifications, many of us struggle to focus on a single task and sustain our attention for more than a few minutes—to an extent that may even be physically rewiring our brains. Studies have shown that multitasking really isn't productive, and even serial tasking with frequent switch-ups—for example, checking your email every few minutes while trying to finish a work presentation—ends up radically lowering productivity because of a concept business professor Sophie Leroy named "attention residue": when you switch from your email back to your task at hand, part of your attention remains with your email, such that there is a significant lag time until you're fully focused on your original task again. So if you keep switching between one task and another, you may never be fully concentrating on what you have to do. I read about one company that calculated the costs of such lost productivity among its workers and discovered it was wasting the equivalent of a Learjet every year. Yikes. And at least in my own case, working like this doesn't feel good. I may feel "busy" (or more accurately, busy-busy-busy), but I don't think I'm especially productive, and I feel ungrounded and discontent.

Speaking of discontent, social media makes it all too easy to feel rotten about yourself or superior to others. It can certainly help us stay in touch with loved ones and reconnect with long-lost high school classmates, but social media can also make us absolutely miserable—even to the point of social media-induced suicide. If you're already feeling bad about your life, all you have to do is check out your Facebook friends' shiny, happy posts, and you will jump fully into the dark pit of envy and despair. Checking "likes," someone put it bitingly, is the new smoking. Social media also allows us to sort ourselves into like-minded tribes and echo chambers, so our indignant rage at those outside our in-group gets encouraged and amplified. Either scenario—invidious comparison or group-think back thumping—ultimately leads to unhappiness. How can we really be happy if we hate the out-group or hate ourselves?

But what about all the great shows on Netflix, or those awesome how-to videos on YouTube? Yes, there is a lot of helpful, high-quality content out there. And it's not that content-bingeing is some kind of an intrinsic evil. It's just that it so easily vacuums up time and steals oxygen from other creative, deeply satisfying pursuits, such as music, art, skilled craft work, bodywork, being outside, writing, relationships, and service.

It seems self-evident that cultivating a life of intentional simplicity means drawing good boundaries around the way we interact with digital communications and social media so that we can make room for other, more helpful ways of spending time. But why is that so hard to do? One reason is that despite all our whiz-bang technological prowess, we are still basically walking around with ancient, hunter-gatherer brains. We are inherently social, with intense tribal loyalties hardwired all the way through our prefrontal cortex and deep down into our limbic system. And so, the dreaded Fear Of Missing Out—that if we set aside our phones and our feeds, the herd will leave us behind and we will be picked off by predators or left to starve and die alone. Of course that's figurative in our day and age, but the cortisol it generates doesn't know the difference between Facebook and the Pleistocene savanna of our ancestors. A corollary of FOMO is the kind of peer-pressure-driven culture we have created, especially in knowledge-work jobs, which sets an expectation that we will be perpetually available and responsive to calls, emails, and texts—even on evenings, weekends, and vacations. We don't want to buck the system, even if the system is making absolutely unreasonable demands on us, because the system is what validates us, gives us a sense of belonging, and signs our paycheck. *But what if the system is crazy?*

Beyond tribalism and peer pressure is something deeply and disturbingly biochemical: addiction. Every time we get an email, a text, a like, or a retweet, every time we watch a video or a show, we get a dopamine hit that activates the pleasure centers of our brain. Yes—just like from drugs or alcohol. And just like drugs or alcohol, that can lead very quickly to addictive behavior. To make it worse and more insidious, the tech companies behind a lot of social media platforms and streaming services design their sites in such a way that encourages behavioral addiction. True, alcohol use doesn't have to end in the wreckage of addiction. I certainly enjoy a nice glass of wine or a snifter of bourbon every now and again, with no ill effect. But digital media platforms are more akin to crystal meth, which is pretty much designed to ruin your life. They are not neutral or harmless, and they are not your friend; they are designed to get you hooked, mine data from you, deliver advertising content, and turn their founders into zillionaires. Didn't we learn that from the January 6, 2021, riots at the Capitol, which were fomented and coordinated through social media? It's not to say you can't use all these digital tools for good, or at least without circling the drain. It's possible, and many people do. But you have to be very careful. You're playing with fire—or more accurately, dynamite.

It's tempting just to throw up our hands and say that the horse has already left the barn and the genie is out of the bottle. It's true that the digital world is here to stay, but for exactly that reason, it's important to do our best to navigate it well. As a species, we may have some inherent tendencies that make us especially vulnerable to all these addictive digital temptations—just as it's so difficult to avoid junk food!—but at the end of the day, we are capable of so much more than the paltry pleasures offered us by the digital realm. How do we work with the digital world in a way that we get the best out of it, don't fall prey to its temptations, and make room for what is deeply satisfying?

## DEEP WORK, FLOW, PRAYER, AND PLEASURE

For one, there is what author and computer scientist Cal Newport calls "deep work," the ability to stay focused while performing a demanding task, especially one that requires a high level of cognitive concentration. This is similar to what psychologist Mihaly Csikszentmihalyi has described as a state of flow, when you are completely absorbed in an activity that entails creativity and skill. When you are in a flow state or doing deep work, you have given yourself fully to what you are doing. You're not checking email or texts or your social media feeds. You're not browsing streaming services for new content. You're not snagging the best deal on Amazon. You're simply doing one thing, whether that is performing a piano concerto, writing a fine paragraph, helping your third-grader with her math, or getting the ignition timing properly set. You have, to borrow a phrase from Thomas Merton, forgotten yourself on purpose. Like Mary, you are truly and fully attentive to the one thing needful, rather than busy with the ten thousand things, like Martha. For me, busy and distracted as I often am, these states tend to come mostly when I'm rock climbing or writing. When I'm climbing up a vertical cliff face 110 feet off the ground, trying to figure out the next handhold or foothold, nothing else matters; there is only the rock. And although writing is often difficult and even torturous for me, I also have plenty of times when I'm deep in the flow of an idea, the right words are coming, and time melts away.

In my experience, there's a very fuzzy line between these kinds of experiences and prayer. In fact, I believe firmly that if approached with intention, such states can indeed be forms of prayer: deep, open attentiveness to the present moment, in which our own egos are emptied out so we have room to be filled with the divine. I find this to be especially true in regard to the creative process. Anyone who does creative work knows that there is an element of gift and receptivity to it. I don't have full control over the words I write. They're given to me, but only if I show up (pretty regularly) with an open heart and open hands. The minute I clench down and think everything is up to me, the flow dries up. Even when I'm climbing, if I try to manhandle things and grasp too hard, my forearms get "pumped" and I blow off the wall (yes, twenty-five-foot falls like this, even with a rope, are their own kind of come-to-Jesus experience). Most things worth doing require a light touch. You just have to trust that the next word will come, that the thin handhold or toehold will indeed hold. You can put yourself in a position to receive, but the gifts come on their own terms. God is not tame. The Spirit blows where and when and how she wills. We dance along.

Such experiences are not just prayer, but also simple pleasure, one of the core themes of this book. I don't really get that excited about having read and responded to umpteen emails in a day, but I get deep satisfaction from having written several hundred words that I believe in, or repairing Cyndi's car, or completing a challenging climb. I also feel soul-deep pleasure when I've tended relationships in an analog way, with live interaction (even if mediated by a cell phone or a video-conference platform) or when I've handwritten a note instead of sending it by text or tweet or email.

## DRAWING GOOD BOUNDARIES

I don't want to frame our interaction with the digital world as an either-or, one-or-zero, black-or-white binary, which is such an ongoing temptation in an age of polarization. As I wrote at the beginning of this chapter, our digital tools can serve good and useful purposes. We just need to engage with them in ways that are conscious and aware, with an appropriate balance between appreciation of their gifts and cautions about their darker sides. How can we bring full intentionality to our relationship with the digital world? How can we interact with such platforms in a way that makes room for us to be truly free—free from distraction and FOMO, free for presence and good work and relationships? Isn't such freedom, after all, always and ever the gift of simplicity?

If we take the addictive nature of the digital realm seriously, becoming free requires, just as in the Twelve Steps, recognizing how powerless we often are in the face of such temptations. From there, rather than shaming ourselves, it's more helpful to start paying close attention to how our use of various media makes us feel. We can be curious, but not judgmental, and discern what is life-giving and what we might want to change.

At this point, it's good to be clear about what kind of relationship you want to have with digital media. And then be ruthless—because at least up to a point, desperate times call for desperate measures. Establish rules, protocols, and structures that will help you. Write them down and articulate them for yourself and for those whom your choices will affect (and whose help and support you'll probably need). If you're really in the throes of digital addiction, you might even undertake a thirty-day "digital detox," in which you disconnect to the maximum extent possible, then resume your relationship with digital media according to the guidelines you've established.

I think it's telling that a lot of tech moguls won't let their kids be on social media platforms, so you might consider just quitting them or engaging with them in a very limited way. I made that move during the ugliness of the 2020 election, and I haven't looked back. If you're going to be on social media, use it as a platform for good—by putting thoughtful, high-quality content out there.

Email is tricky. Since most of us have to use it, you can't just walk away. But you also don't have to be a slave to it. You can turn off all notifications on all your devices, and just check manually at specific times of the day and week. This allows you to schedule blocks of time to do uninterrupted deep work, and if you only check work email during work hours, to draw some boundaries around work. You don't *have* to respond to every single email or always respond promptly either. This might occasionally mean declaring "email bankruptcy" or dealing with the fallout from a neglected message, but in my experience, many messages that seem important at the time often resolve themselves or fade in priority.

One of the best pandemic lockdown memes I heard about was three simple words: "I finished Netflix." Most of us are suckers for online content delivery, so it can be helpful to give yourself a time budget or otherwise have some routines that will help you limit your intake to something reasonable. Whenever I open YouTube to find something useful, I have to consciously remind myself to be careful, knowing how easy it is for me to get sucked in.

Finally, try to make room for a lot of digital-free time and space in your life. For me, this means not keeping any device in the bedroom and not using any digital device for at least an hour after waking up. Some commit to a "digital Sabbath," a time each week or month with no devices or internet connectivity.

Your circumstances will dictate what works best for you, and your practices will probably evolve, as mine have. The point is setting the boundaries in the first place, and then following through as best you can.

## CRAFTING OUR TIME

There's a wonderful upside to such disciplined vigilance: the possibility of becoming true craftsmen and craftswomen of the time we're given. We all know that we only have so much of it. We can't get it back or create more. We can only make good choices about how we steward it, and the ubiquity of digital media can make that a real challenge. If you're on the spiritual path of simplicity, however, it's a worthy challenge, because embedded within it is the chance to make—or to allow God to make—something truly beautiful of your life. Again, on the far side of structure, discipline, and good boundaries lies a spaciousness in which you can experience freedom, truly prayerful presence, self-acceptance, creativity, and meaningful connections—not on Mark Zuckerberg's terms, but on your own.

# ten

# RUGGED INTERDEPENDENCE

I was idealistic in a way that you can only be in your twenties when I bought a piece of land that would become a home and farm. My head was filled with the lovely poetry, inspiring fiction, and razor-sharp essays of the agrarian writer Wendell Berry, a role model and mentor to me. Inspired also by Henry David Thoreau, I had Walden-like visions of a life stripped down to its barest essentials, a hand-built life with such basic needs that a simple livelihood would suffice to support it, leaving time and mental space for reflection, writing, prayer, and other noble pursuits. I would unplug from the Matrix, free myself of distractions, and think my own thoughts. I would become, as Ralph Waldo Emmerson recommended, self-reliant.

I didn't quite go down the doomsday prepper rabbit hole and load up on dried food, guns, and ammunition. But I did seek to separate myself somewhat from the machinery of the American capitalist system. I had in mind the ideal of the independent landholder, whose freedom comes from not being utterly beholden to the larger economy. I saw so much of that economy as corrupt, largely run by the wealthy for the benefit of the wealthy. I also wondered whether the machine would be able to keep running, as it devoured at an absolutely ferocious rate the natural capital on which it depended. I may not have thought too much about utter collapse, but I could very easily imagine how our economy's long, complex supply chains could be vulnerable to disruption, and I wanted to build some resilience into my life. Even if it didn't free me from some kind of ultimate dependence on the larger economy, at least it might give me some breathing room and some perspective. As Upton Sinclair once put it, "It is difficult to get a man to understand something when his salary depends upon his not understanding it." I didn't want my salary to put a ring in my nose and blinkers on my eyes.

## SIMPLICITY ISN'T SO SIMPLE

Like most of my ideals, however, this ideal of simple independence crashed quickly and mercilessly on the shoals of reality. Because if you want to farm, you can't do it with just a digging stick. You need farming equipment, and that costs money. If you want to build a house, you need tools and materials, which also require capital. I lusted after a bright orange Kubota and shiny new equipment, but what I could actually afford was a fifty-year-old tractor that broke down all the time and farm implements that fell apart if I looked at them the wrong way. Though I had saved up some cash to build a simple barn and finish out part of it as a bachelor-pad apartment, the burn rate of my savings was so breathtaking that I needed to find a full-time job off the farm to keep the farm bankrolled. With a sinking feeling—you know, like your ideals sinking into the swamp of your actual life—I began to understand that the kind of small-scale organic farming and homesteading I'd dreamt about as a vocation was far more likely to end up as an expensive hobby rather than a solid primary income. There's a joke about a farmer who won the lottery, and when asked what he would do with the money, said he'd just keep farming until it was all gone. I began to slide more quickly down the slippery slope into the very kinds of entanglements I'd set out to avoid.

I was learning a hard truth: back-to-the-land simplicity is actually very complicated. Within six months of purchasing my land, I had resigned myself to farming and building in the off-hours alongside my full-time professional job, a twenty-minute drive away. Instead of meeting my simplified needs with just twenty hours a week on the farm, having plenty of spare time to cultivate a life of deep prayer and reflection, I found myself working forty hours a week off the farm, and working another forty or more hours on the farm—early mornings, late evenings, and weekends. How did *that* happen?

And that was before meeting Cyndi, getting married, having children, and building, just two years after finishing the barn/bachelor-pad apartment, an honest-to-goodness house.

The need for even a modest income wasn't the only complicating factor, though it was a big one. The other piece of it—or more accurately, the many other pieces of it—was that the kind of life I was trying to lead required a huge array of skills, practically none of which I had learned growing up. My parents were educated professionals with busy white-collar jobs, not fourth-generation farmers who had taught me how to butcher chickens or diagnose a bad bearing in a bush hog. I had to learn these things mostly on my own—and mostly by a lot of trial and error. After I built our home, I used to joke—after enough time had passed for me to develop a sense of humor about it—that I hadn't built one house, but about three, because I had to do almost every step three times before I got it right. I had to learn concrete work, framing, plumbing, wiring, insulation, roofing, and finish carpentry—oh, and welding, mechanics, soil science, forestry management, canning and drying, and.... Each one of those skills also required some specialty tools and equipment, which I had to buy, rent, or borrow.

Don't get me wrong: I really loved learning all these things. It felt satisfying in a primal way that I can't adequately explain, and I'm still grateful for those skills. At the same time, it also added up to a lot of hours, a lot of dollars, and a lot of disappointment at how difficult and complicated simplicity was turning out to be. For the sake of a simple life, I had tried to unplug from the complicated machine of the modern American economy. But I had ended up just taking on a lot of that complexity myself—partly out of principle, but mostly, if I'm honest, because I was too proud, too stubborn, and too cheap to pay other people to do what I felt I could figure out how to do myself. I had thought simplicity and self-sufficiency were synonymous. I was wrong.

## THE MYTH OF RUGGED INDEPENDENCE

The missing variable in all of this was *other people*. One of the absolutely crucial things I learned over the years on the farm was that self-sufficiency is the wrong goal. I think my instincts were right to critique the economic ideal of the American consumer, who needn't bother knowing how her home is built or heated, how his food comes to his plate, where her clothing comes from, or where his garbage goes— simply because he or she can write checks or use credit cards. It's certainly convenient, and you can definitely save space by not owning any do-it-yourself tools. But that kind of dependence on the system and on the anonymous people who make it work seems like a recipe for feeling vulnerable, disempowered, and lonely. On the other hand, the opposite of such dependency is its own form of madness, whether it takes the form of being a jack of all trades, as I tried to be, or a hermit mountain man, living on roots and berries, beholden to no one (at least until he gets hurt or sick or old). Whether we acknowledge it or not, we are a social, interconnected species living in webs of relationships. Rugged independence is a myth, or else a very particular form of hell.

Eventually, I let go of the idea of rugged independence, realizing it was a wrong turn from the path of simple living. Instead, I began to put stock in the practice of rugged *inter-dependence*. Even though I am far from the farm and the farming life in which I learned that practice, I still think it is a far more beautiful, sustainable, human, and enjoyable way to live out the vocation of simplicity.

The "rugged" part of rugged interdependence takes seriously that most of us have become radically and dangerously disconnected from almost every basic process that sustains our life and provides us our goods and services. Because of the way our money-based, globalized economy works, it's now possible to become über-specialized in one particular thing—say, computer programming, for example—and to use the money you earn from that job to buy every single other good or service that sustains your life, with no idea of what—and who—is behind the curtain. Such a degree of disconnection is a great risk: What happens if even one cog in the whole machine breaks down, as we have learned in the pandemic? I still remember, as you probably do, going to the grocery store early in the pandemic, seeing all the bare shelves and feeling lucky to go home with even a few essentials. We learned that it's hard to be resilient when we're so helplessly dependent on the system working perfectly. It's also hard to critique the system: How inclined are you to bite the hand that feeds you? And I think if we're honest, for all the convenience and luxury that our economic system provides—at least to those who have a steady income and don't experience discrimination—there's something deep-down that just doesn't feel good about being that dependent. Not only can it be terrifying, like those empty shelves at the grocery store, but it's also disempowering. We human beings were made to have some hand in meeting our basic needs. It's part of our divine vocation, and it's hardwired into our hunter-gatherer brains and bodies. To be fully human is to take some part, however small, in providing for our own sustenance.

The kind of ruggedness I'm talking about certainly won't and doesn't have to look like homesteading on a small farm (though I still hope to return to some older, wiser, lighter-duty version of that at some point). There are plenty of ways to be "rugged" in the sense of reconnecting in a tangible way with some of our more basic needs. For many people, it probably means taking more ownership in food production—perhaps growing a garden, raising chickens in the backyard, purchasing more locally grown food, almost certainly doing more cooking. More on this in another chapter. Perhaps rugged looks like taking on more home repair or car maintenance. It might entail installing a rain barrel on your house, or a solar power system, or some other locally appropriate technologies. Maybe rugged takes the form of walking or biking to work rather than hopping in the car. For me, living in a rural area, one big part of rugged is making firewood to heat our home. Rugged will always mean taking account of your own skills and interests, as well as consulting the "genius of the place" to make best use of what is near at hand, which has always been the driver of real sustainability.

The whole "reskilling" movement has recognized that many of the domestic arts of home economics are in danger of being lost, as the generations who regularly practiced them die off. In this respect, thank goodness for YouTube and the internet. Learning a skill from a YouTube video is a far cry from apprenticing to your grandma, but at least it keeps the skill alive when the person-to-person knowledge transmission network falters.

The point is not exactly what you do, or what percentage of your needs you manage to meet with your own hand. Realistically, for most of us, that percentage will be very low. But the difference between making no effort and making some effort is huge. When you make room in your life for activities that meet some of your own needs, you connect with the Zen ideal of "chopping wood and carrying water"— namely, immersing yourself in small, practical, concrete daily tasks that keep you grounded, keep you humble, and can be the place of profound revelation about yourself and the world around you. It's deep commitment to these kinds of things that can help you see the sacredness in your everyday world. You also tend to have a smaller environmental footprint when you try to meet your needs closer to home. And almost inevitably, you come to a deep awareness of how much it actually takes to support your middle-class, developed-country life.

That can lead to gratitude for the wonder of it all, but it can also lead to an awareness of how privileged and fragile it is and how proactive you may need to become in order to have a bit more resilience. I remember one time back on the farm, a bad snowstorm knocked out power and stranded everyone in their home for several days. Knowing that we had young kids, one of our neighbors made his way over to our place on his tractor to check on us. Because we ran on solar power, had our own water supply, heated our home with a woodstove, and kept plenty of food on hand, we had hardly blinked at the disruption. In fact, we were out sledding when he came by, and I actually felt bad because we were getting along more easily than he himself was. It's powerfully freeing to not be completely and utterly beholden to the system.

We are beholden, however. And we should be—just not to an anonymous system, but to other people, on whom we depend and who depend on us. We are made to be rugged, but ruggedness only goes so far without interdependence.

If I learned a lot of ruggedness from farming, I also learned that I couldn't do it all myself. Whenever I got my tractor hopelessly stuck, a neighbor would come and pull me out. When we were pouring concrete or setting roof trusses or doing other work that could only be done with many hands, friends and neighbors showed up to help. When my wife gave birth to our twins, right in the middle of the hardest part of our home construction, a colleague at work coordinated a food brigade such that we didn't cook a meal ourselves for six weeks. I didn't and couldn't keep track of the favors. I did my best to pay them back or pay them forward, but even so, I felt constantly—and wonderfully—indebted. In that flow of generosity around simple and necessary tasks of meeting core needs, I felt like our family was being woven into the fabric of the place. This is what belonging felt like, and thank goodness, it (mostly) transcended our many differences in terms of politics, educational background, parenting styles, and so forth.

I continue to believe that it's possible to buck the trend of atomization and anonymity and to build or rebuild the structures of communal support that contribute to resilience, empowerment, freedom, local self-sufficiency, and the soul-deep pleasure of connecting in basic ways around basic needs. New systems are emerging to share tools, to buy cooperatively in bulk, and to make it easier to offer and receive skilled and unskilled help and care. My sister-in-law and brother-in-law have some version of this out in a small town in Kansas, where they live in a walkable, tightly knit neighborhood and take part in home-brew cooperative childcare and homeschooling, community gardening, and hand-me-down clothing exchanges. A work colleague of mine has lived for many years in an intentional community of sorts with several families on his street in Louisville. From Shane Claiborne's Simple Way community in Philadelphia to Nazareth Farm in West Virginia to the various Catholic Worker farms and communities scattered across the nation and the world, people are experimenting with new ways of being together, of being with and for one another, centered on simple, common needs—which are strikingly similar to very old ways of being with and for each other, much like the early Christians and the monastics throughout the centuries. To devise these kinds of interdependent relational networks is, to my mind, a wonderful and necessary new form of creativity.

Rugged interdependence does, however, take time. It certainly takes the time that a more hands-on kind of life requires. But far more importantly, it takes time—a *lot* of time—to tend to reciprocal relationships. On so many occasions when I was in the middle of a farm project, I needed to borrow something from our neighbor Jack in order to finish it. The borrowing would inevitably involve twenty minutes of shooting the breeze when I picked it up, and another twenty minutes when I returned it. It was the cost of doing business, this making room in a busy day for real interactions that led to real relationships. Sometimes, it was a maddening cost, when I was in a hurry and just wanted to finish something. Now that Jack has passed on, though, I can hardly remember the particular projects I was trying to get done with his help. But I do remember the kind, caring person Jack was. I carry the stories he told, and I carry the stories *I* tell about his and my various misadventures. That's only possible because we made room for each other; we invested time in each other, just like I'm willing to spend far more time on a project so that my kids can do it with me, in their own way and at their own pace.

It will always be quicker and easier and more convenient—as long as The Economy keeps on humming—to sustain our lives just by swiping credit cards and writing checks, paying people we don't know for things we can't do or make ourselves, and sustaining the illusion of our separateness from one another. It will also be lonelier, less satisfying, less free, and less resilient. Part of a simpler life entails seeing through that hollow kind of faux simplicity and, ironically, choosing to take on a deeper, richer kind of complexity as we reconnect more intentionally and competently with what it actually takes to sustain our lives. Simplicity isn't self-sufficiency or the Daniel Boone ideal of rugged independence. It's the beautiful, time-consuming privilege of rugged interdependence, when we roll up our sleeves with and for others in a great community of needful belonging.

# eleven

# FOOD

We all need to eat. For that simple reason of physical survival, food is ever-present in our lives. We can at least imagine scenarios where we could manage without using money. But not food. We can't live long without it, and most of us deal with food several times a day, every day. It's one of the most important realms in our life where a commitment to simplicity can play out.

I love food. I've had a big appetite for as long as I can remember, and I love a fairly wide variety of foods, which is a great relief to my mom, because when I was a kid, I was a picky, meat-and-potatoes eater who had to be fooled into eating vegetables by her clever efforts to disguise them. Then, in college I started dating someone who was a foodie vegetarian, which blew the doors of my culinary world wide open. That relationship didn't last long, but the appreciation for food that it engendered in me has remained, almost three decades later. Shoot, I love food so much that I had intended to spend my life as an organic farmer, growing it.

## FOOD AND OUR BODIES, OUR SOCIETY, OUR WORLD

Each one of us has a relationship with food that's intensely individual and personal—and complicated. Food gives life to our bodies, and making good food choices is one of the most fundamental things we can to do promote our health and longevity. At least to me, there are few greater pleasures than partaking of food I really enjoy. Some of my best memories are associated with meals and comfort foods. And yet what can give us such pleasure can also be the source of temptation and pathology. According to a recent Harvard study, more than 70 percent of Americans are overweight, including 40 percent of Americans who are obese—so it's clear that a lot of us have a problematic relationship with food. Add in those who struggle with anorexia, bulimia, and other eating disorders. Almost all of us have some issues with body-image and self-esteem, and food is nearly always at play. It can be a real stumbling block. I've noticed this especially since the coronavirus pandemic hit. Pre-pandemic, when I went to an office every day, I always had a meeting-crammed schedule, and I didn't think much about eating, other than at lunch. Now that I'm working mostly from home, each trip past the fridge or pantry is a small test of willpower, and let's just say that I haven't been passing with flying colors.

Eating is never just personal, though. The social dimension of food is obvious in the meals we eat with our families and with friends, with clients and coworkers, on the shy first date, at the wedding reception or the funeral potluck. Sharing food is in large part how we share life with one another. Eating together binds us to one another, gives us a sense of belonging, offers us common memories and a common identity.

Food also binds us to others well beyond those who might share our table. Unless we grow and cook all our own food, to eat means to take part in a complicated system that generally starts in a farmer's field or feed lot or a fishery (perhaps on the other side of the globe) and runs through a long chain of transportation, processing, storage, and distribution before it ends up in the retail grocery or the restaurant where you encounter it. With more regionally based food systems, many of those steps may be simplified, such as when a farmer sells directly to customers at a farm market or through a community-supported agriculture subscription. For better or worse, and to paraphrase a line from Walt Whitman, the food we eat contains multitudes. Food contains the honest hard work of the farmer, but also the exploited labor of the underpaid illegal farm worker and, as we've learned in the pandemic, the grocery workers who are somehow both essential and expendable at the same time. It contains the privilege enjoyed by those of us who can frequent good grocery stores, and also the injustice experienced by those who can't afford nutritious food or who live in "food deserts" (usually in blighted urban areas) with no easy access to well-stocked grocery shelves. It contains the federal agriculture policies and subsidy programs that tend to favor large agribusiness corporations, whose far-reaching seed patents and armies of lawyers often make it difficult or impossible for smaller-scale farmers (especially in developing countries) to compete and survive. Whether we eat alone or with others, our food choices affect many human lives besides our own.

How we eat affects the life of the more-than-human world too. Eating isn't just personal and social; it's also an ecological act. Eating ties us inextricably to the many biological systems that sustain life on this planet. Unfortunately, most modern food production is fundamentally destructive of the natural systems on which it depends. Agriculture and grazing are largely responsible for a great deal of deforestation, including the destruction of rain forests and other critical, biodiverse habitats. Overfishing has drastically depleted fish stocks. Inefficient, large-scale crop irrigation dries up rivers and drains ancient aquifers. Poor farming methods degrade the soil and erode it up to twenty times faster than nature can build it back up. At current rates of erosion, we'll have no more topsoil in just sixty years. Fertilizers, herbicides, and pesticides end up in waterways and in the bodies of birds and bees and frogs—and humans. Billions of our animal kin suffer miserable lives and painful deaths in the confined animal feeding operations that supply much of our meat. And in all of this, the agriculture sector—especially raising animals for meat—generates more planet-warming greenhouse gases than all forms of land, air, and water transportation combined.

Every time we eat, we contribute—positively or negatively—to the health of our bodies, our society, and the rest of the living world. In practically no other area of our life do our mundane daily choices have such significant, tangible effects. It's also a daily invitation to go deeper with our spiritual life.

## SPIRITUALITY AND FOOD

Food plays a significant role in religious traditions. Jews celebrate the Passover Seder to remember the Hebrew exodus from Egypt, and the Hebrew Scriptures tell how the Jewish people were sustained in the desert by manna given them directly by God. The weekly Shabbat meals anchor Jewish life in a rhythm of work and rest, and keeping kosher is an important part of many Jewish households. Food offerings are an ancient ritual in Buddhism, and there are similar offerings in Shinto and Hindu traditions. Muslims celebrate the Iftar dinner to break the daily Ramadan fast and, like Jews, were given guidelines by the Koran about certain foods, such as pork, to avoid as part of their religious devotion. For Christians, much of Jesus's life and ministry centered on food and table fellowship. He attended countless dinners and parties, he ate with leading religious figures, he miraculously fed thousands, and on the eve of his crucifixion, he shared a last supper with his disciples where he instituted the central practice of Christian faith, the Eucharist. After his resurrection, he shared food with his disciples as proof that he really was alive again.

It makes a lot of sense that food would factor so heavily into religious devotion. Like breathing, eating is something you have to do on a regular basis in order to stay alive. But also like breathing, you can eat without much thought or consideration, or you can bring awareness and intentionality into the process. If the true purpose of religion is to connect us (literally, to "re-ligament" us) consciously to the divine presence in all things, then eating is a perfect opportunity to make room for that awareness. Like the air we breathe, the food we eat is ultimately a gift. We certainly have to do our part: as the Catholic Eucharistic Prayers put it, bread is the fruit of the earth *and* the work of human hands. But as any farmer or gardener will tell you, the work of human hands, however hard that work may be, is never enough. You can do your best to create all the right conditions for things to grow, but in the end, you're not in charge. Whether you're picking wild greens in the woods or picking peppers from your garden, any harvest is a gift beyond human control. And at least to me, any gift beyond human control is an invitation to acknowledge and give thanks to the Giver of all good things.

Food, then, offers a constant opportunity to take in gifts with gratitude, which is one of the fundamental practices of the spiritual life. Every time you eat is a chance to give thanks for all those many links in the great chain of being that brings nourishment to your body and your soul. It's a chance to be grateful for the miracle of your body, which can take food and turn it into the miracle that is you or, if you are pregnant, your developing child. There are plenty of times when I take food for granted, when I treat it merely as fuel, or when, to use one of the phrases I like least in the English language, I just "grab a bite." But other times, whether it's in receiving the Eucharist or eating Cyndi's homemade pizza on Friday nights, I'm full—of wonder, gratitude, and a sense of belonging with those I eat with and with the beautiful living world that brings such miracles to my plate. Saying grace over meals, then eating with full awareness and intention, is one of the most profoundly spiritual practices I know of—and we have a chance to do it several times, every day.

Because eating has so many physical, psychological, social, ecological, and spiritual dimensions, it's also one of the most consequential practices to which we can bring the values of simplicity. It can also be one of the hardest areas to consistently stick to your convictions. As with all things in the simplicity journey, we do the best we can.

## EATING MEAT

One of the biggest decisions we can make in regard to eating with simplicity is where on the food chain we choose to eat—namely, the amount and kinds of meat and other animal products we want in our diet. More than any other food choice we might make, this has the most far-reaching social and environmental impact. A meat-heavy diet has more than twice the carbon footprint of a diet without any animal products, and among animal products, beef and lamb have almost four times more environmental impact than chicken, fish, or pork, about three times more impact than dairy, and almost eleven times more impact than breads and grains. Because "environmental impact" and "carbon footprint" are abstract terms, what such impact looks like in practice is, for example, much of the Brazilian rain forest being cut down in order to use that land for grazing cattle or raising soybeans to feed cattle. And in addition to environmental impact is the fact that almost all animals raised for meat are raised in cruel, inhumane conditions. When we eat animals who are treated this way, we may not be doing the torturing and killing ourselves, but we are supporting it with our food dollars—and though I can't prove it, I believe we are "eating anger," as the Buddhist monk Thich Nhat Hanh puts it—we absorb into ourselves some of the violence inherent in that process.

In general, then, simplifying our eating would mean eating less (or no) meat, leaning toward pork and poultry and fish for the meat that we do eat, and trying to source our meat as humanely and sustainably as possible. For example, it's possible to raise cattle in a way that is kind to the animals, encourages their natural grazing and herd instincts, improves the soil, and sequesters carbon. It's possible to buy pasture-raised chickens or turkeys (or to raise them yourself), or to eat sustainably raised or wild-caught fish. These options are going to be more expensive, no doubt. That will mean spending a larger percentage of your income on food—which, to my mind, isn't a bad thing, if you're able to swing it, compared to other things we often spend money on. Or it may mean that you may not be able to have meat quite as frequently. Once upon a time, after all, meat was considered a luxury—and still is in many poorer parts of the world.

Though I was a vegetarian for many years, Cyndi's physiology is such that she does better with a bit of meat in her diet, and our kids like it as well, so while we don't each much meat in our household, we do eat some. When we were on the farm, I raised and butchered chickens. We also buy a bit of beef from a friend who is an organic dairy farmer, when he retires animals from his milking herd. We do occasionally buy some poultry and pork from the grocery store—not always, I'm sorry to admit, perfectly in line with the principles sketched out above. And when we're someone else's guests, receiving their hospitality trumps pretty much any other principle. We eat what's put in front of us.

I do think we evolved as omnivores (why else would we have canine teeth?) and that there's a good case to be made for eating some meat—especially fish, and especially in cases where land is too steep to be farmed but could be safely grazed.

But there's no denying that however thoughtfully you may eat meat, you are willingly doing fatal violence (even if indirectly) to another sentient creature. Again, I think that violence is a part of the circle of life, and if you're going to take part in it, at least do it with full awareness and good intention. I try to do that as a deer hunter, following First Nations' principles of the Honorable Harvest by asking the deer to give herself or himself for our family's needs, making a clean kill at close range with a single shot of my bow or rifle, giving thanks and showing deep respect to the animal, taking only what is required for our freezer, and doing all the processing myself. All that said, I still think that with the human population being as large as it is, many more of us could cut back a lot or entirely on our meat consumption. For myself, I can definitely envision a time when I give up hunting or even give up meat again completely. As in all things on the journey of simplicity, ongoing discernment is the name of the game.

## EATING OUT

Another big question to discern is that of eating out or eating in. I honestly feel that fast-food dining doesn't deserve much of a place in an intentionally simple lifestyle. It certainly seems like the simplest thing in the world to run in to (or drive through) McDonald's and "grab a bite." But there is a lot of complicated machinery behind what seems so simple, and hardly any of it is just or sustainable, from ecological impact to animal welfare to palm-oil plantations to the wage-slave labor of fast-food employees. When my family and I are on the road, we often pack meals or improvise at grocery stores, or we try to find restaurants that seem at least somewhat aligned with our values. At the very least, I try to eat lower on the food chain in such situations. But I don't like the way I feel, body or soul, when I eat much fast food.

Not all restaurants serve fast food, of course. Cyndi, far more than I, loves eating out in nice restaurants. She loves the chance to try new dishes. She loves the atmosphere. Perhaps most importantly, since she is the primary cook in our household, she loves getting a break from the daily responsibilities of putting meals on the table for a hungry family of five. I don't mind restaurant dining, but between our limited household budget and my own skinflint tendencies, I struggle to enjoy it as much as she does. I often find myself doing mental calculations about what the price of a meal could have otherwise purchased, or what good it could have done if donated, or what it could have earned if we'd invested it in our retirement account. Cyndi often remarks that such tendencies don't make it especially fun to go out to eat with me, so I try my best to keep such observations to myself. I do think that there are some amazing restaurants that work hard to serve really high-quality food and support local farmers. I have friends whose daughter and son-in-law started such an enterprise. Our general rule of thumb is that good restaurants—especially unique, locally owned establishments—are a wonderful splurge, reserved for birthdays and anniversaries and other special occasions. Your budget and your own convictions may lead you to different conclusions.

## COOKING SIMPLY

If the pandemic has done anything positive, it's that it has sent many of us back to the kitchen, both because restaurants are less accessible and because many of us have more time on our hands. In that respect, our family was about as pandemic-prepared as anyone, because we are a cook-from-scratch, eat-together kind of household, with a lot of dry beans and grains on hand, as well as a large chest freezer with a year's supply of frozen garden produce, blueberries, meat, and other items. In our household, family dinner is sacrosanct. It's always been the axle on which our days turn, the center that draws us each back in from the centrifugal force of whatever has happened that day.

Not every household will cook as frequently or intensively as we do (just to be clear once again, so I don't claim any credit where it's not due: Cyndi is the head cook in our household, and my role is generally pretty minimal). But I think that making room in your schedule to center the process of cooking and eating at home is one of the most profound steps toward simplicity that it's possible to take. You certainly don't have to be a gourmet chef, have a $50,000 kitchen with fancy appliances and copious cabinetry, or stock your fridge and pantry full of exotic ingredients.

Good meals do start with good ingredients, though, and my favorite place to go for them is our garden. When I'm harvesting a fresh cucumber or clipping kale to put in a breakfast smoothie a few minutes later, I often find myself thinking that no amount of wealth could possibly procure better, fresher food than what comes out of a low-budget, unpretentious kitchen garden. For those fortunate enough to have a bit of land or have access to community garden space, one of the best blessings I know of is fresh, in-season produce. When we were on the farm, I grew huge gardens, and we filled fridge, freezer, root cellar, bellies, and our neighbors' front porches with utterly unreasonable amounts of fresh produce. I even tried my hand at growing wheat, which we sowed by hand, harvested with hedge clippers, threshed with bedsheets and plastic baseball bats, winnowed in front of a box fan, then ground into flour (and no, I will never take a kernel of wheat for granted again). We still have a decent-sized garden at our current place, but it's a lot smaller and provides a much lower percentage of our calories. While I don't necessarily miss the amount of labor that I had to invest on our previous place, I sure do miss the amount and variety of food we were able to grow. But regardless of whether you're *Mother Earth News*-worthy self-sufficient or just growing a few tomatoes in a pot on your balcony, or even just sprouts in a jar on your countertop, there are few more satisfying things than being able to put at least some amount of food on your table that you grew yourself. Something deep in the prehistoric parts of the brain thrums with gladness and pleasure at the ability to provide in this way, to add the work of our hands to the divine gift of growth, delivered through the forces of nature. I also feel a deep solidarity with the rest of the human race, across geography, culture, and time. Many generations of human beings have had a direct hand in procuring food, and I can't help but feeling that our current situation, with more than half of the human population living in cities and having little or no chance to produce food, is an evolutionary wrong turn.

That's our situation, though, and even gardeners generally aren't able to grow all their own food (although biointensive gardener John Jeavons proved that if you're really skilled and willing to put in the effort, you can grow all the calories a person needs for a year on about four thousand square feet of garden space). But for the many people who aren't able or inclined to garden this intensively or at all, where does simple cooking start?

When it's possible, it's great to start at the source and purchase as much as you can directly from local farmers. The platonic ideal of this is to buy a share in a community-supported agriculture (CSA) subscription, where for some up-front money to the farmer, you get a season's supply of produce—and perhaps also meat, dairy, and other products—delivered weekly to a central drop-off site. In good years, you share the surplus, and in bad years, you take the hit with the farmer. It's a beautiful way to re-localize the agricultural economy.

Another option is to frequent local farmers markets. As with the CSA, the logistics of shopping at farmers markets can be really tricky. You have to go during certain hours on a certain day, and you usually pay premium prices. But like the CSA, a farmers market can be a really powerful way to build community with other shoppers and with the farmers themselves. I have my doubts that they are scalable in a way that can compete in a meaningful way with agribusiness. But when they work, they are human commerce at its best.

You may not always (or ever) be able to get food directly from a local farmer. But why let the perfect be the enemy of the good? There's a whole lot of daylight between growing things yourself or purchasing directly from local farmers, on the one hand, and having the Amazon truck drop off a box full of goodies from God knows where and God knows whom, on the other. Back in college and graduate school, my favorite grocery shopping experiences were co-op grocery stores where I could buy in bulk, often score products from local farmers, and hang around cool foody people, hoping some of their vibe would rub off on me. I still hold out hope for a day when small-scale farmers band together into cooperatives that can pool resources in a way that can effectively compete with Big Ag, at scale. Presently, my family and I don't have easy access to co-op groceries, so we procure a lot of our food-stuffs mainly from the local chain grocery. We also order a lot of bulk grains and beans through internet retailers. When we do go to the grocery store, we try to avoid most processed or pre-prepared food—it's not only unhealthy and designed to be addictive, but it's just got no soul to it. We don't purchase everything organic, but we try to buy a fair amount, as well as get locally sourced and seasonally available produce when we can. Even so, we spend a good chunk of our household budget on food, and I think it's worth it to get good ingredients. The extra we spend really isn't that much compared to what we could spend on even a few restaurant meals, much less the medical expenses of managing diabetes, heart disease, or other chronic problems that a good diet can often prevent.

The magic really happens in the kitchen. But before waxing poetic about cooking—especially when I do so little of it myself these days—I should acknowledge that there's a mundane relentlessness to cooking that can easily turn it into a burden. Plenty of days, plenty of meals, it's hard to bring gratitude to the responsibility of keeping yourself and others fed. On the other hand, I bend the knee to what Cyndi is able to do in the kitchen. Cooking is one of the ways in which she expresses her creativity—our plates are her tapestry. She's also much braver than I ever have been as a cook, trying new recipes from different ethnicities, incorporating whatever I haul in from the garden, and often finding ways to substitute healthier ingredients in favorite old recipes. But she isn't abstemious; while I get a little too uptight about fat and calories, she's unapologetic about her use of butter, whole milk, cream, and cheese. Sometimes I get the notion that I'm going to give up sugar and stop eating desserts—maybe just have a piece of fruit instead. And then Cyndi unveils her latest gluten-free or ancient-grain creation, and any willpower I have dissolves. We don't have desserts every night, but when we do—wow, they make life worth living.

For Cyndi, food is a primary language of love. It's one of the daily ways she shows us how much she cares about us and about the world. Eating is certainly a way to help create the kind of social and ecological world you'd like your grandchildren to inherit. It's a daily opportunity for mindfulness, for gratitude, for responsible stewardship, for simplicity. In the end, though, one of the greatest gifts of food is fellowship. If we really commit to making room in our lives for cooking and eating with intention, food can knit us not just to the blessed living world, but especially to one another. Our family's most joyful and pleasurable moments, and the strongest and most durable bonds, have been forged around the sacred space of our dining table—those thousands upon thousands of hours in which we've shared the contents of our days, offered up our struggles and thanksgivings, laughed with and at each other, dreamed of new possibilities. That's the great gift of being intentional with food: it invites you ever deeper into relationship with the Earth and with your fellow human travelers.

# twelve

# RELATIONSHIPS

I n an earlier chapter, I wrote that dealing with money was
the hard stuff. That's true, but I saved the absolute hardest—
and best—topic for this last chapter. "It's complicated" is
a cultural meme now, often referring to relationships. So if
relationships are by definition complicated, is there a way to
approach them through the lens of simplicity? I think so. In
fact, I think making room for meaningful relationships is the
ultimate end—and means—of a simple, intentional life.

## MADE OF RELATIONSHIPS, MADE FOR RELATIONSHIPS
Before we get too far along, I'd like to clarify what I mean
by relationships. Forgive me if I get excessively biological,
ecological, sociological, and even theological, but it's complicated, right? The simple version of all that complication is
that we're made *of* relationships, and we're made *for* relationships. If we've learned anything from modern science—
both hard science and social science, from neurobiology to
quantum physics to cultural anthropology—it's that the nature

of reality itself is relationship. This is true all the way down to the quantum level, where subatomic particles exist only in relationship with one another. It's true, so the astrophysicists tell us, on the large scale of solar systems, galaxies, and the entire fabric of the known (and much unknown) universe. It's true in our individual biology: our own bodies, our very selves, are a living community of cells, bacteria, and other creatures all living in magnificent if sometimes uneasy symbiosis. It's true in the sense of ecological systems: our individual selves, and our species, don't and can't exist separately from the forests and soil and crops and oceans and atmosphere. In the social realm, we poor mammals are born helpless, and we depend on our parents for an extended period of time—and while we may grow out of that specific dependency of childhood, we never outgrow our need of one another for our emotional and physical well-being. And I believe that reality is this way because everything and everyone is an ongoing creation of God, whose own nature is relationship, who creates the world in the divine image and sustains it through the power of relationships.

It's important to let that last paragraph really sink in, because although the language of relationship, interconnection, and interdependence is starting to get a real foothold in many fields of inquiry, we're still living—at least in America—with a functional epistemology of individualism. Our current educational system, our economic system, much of our popular culture, and basically all of our knowledge grid still operate according to the assumption—the *false* assumption—that we are disconnected individuals, acting rationally of our own free will, maximizing our own benefit, often in zero-sum competition against others. Living a life of intentional simplicity is an attempt to buck these systems—not just to be ornery, but because *they're built on a lie* about human nature and the nature of all reality. The wrongness of these systems and their assumptions has given us runaway climate change, massive wealth inequality, the elderly locked away in facilities, epic loneliness and its attendant pathologies, racial injustices, and so many other ills.

## LEANING INTO RELATIONSHIPS

Simplicity, while it may have moral elements to it, isn't a performance. It's not something you do in order to feel righteous or to get a good grade on divine or human scorecards. In fact, you could live a pitch-perfect, irreproachably simple life, checking all the right boxes, and still be miserable and wretched if you do so in a way that feeds your fear, anger, judgment, narcissism, and ego. Because in the end, simplicity isn't about you. It's about you-in-relationship, which of course is the only real you there is. The point of living simply, then, is that simplicity helps you see through the lie of individualism, and it makes room in your heart so that you can give yourself fully and willingly to your relationships.

Relationships are the source of our deepest longings, most sublime joys, most painful wounds, and most profound griefs. Relationships are indeed complicated—and they are the main point of being alive, because they are what it means even to be alive in the first place. So how can simplicity help you lean deeply into that reality? How can simplicity help you bring your best, most authentic, most loving, most vulnerable, most courageous self to the daily reality of your relationships?

## PRESENCE AND ATTENTIVENESS

We're all so woven into the web of the world that it's impossible to separate ourselves from our relationships. But it's very possible to forget or ignore or deny our connections to others and to the rest of the living world, and in these, to God. It's possible to become alienated and estranged in our relationships. Cyndi and I, like probably every other married couple, go through periods when we feel distant and disconnected from each other. Some of it may just be the natural ebb and flow of any relationship, or the cycles of her mood or mine. But often the chasm grows because one of us (usually me) has become preoccupied and inattentive to the other person. During these times, Cyndi will tell me that although I'm physically there, I'm really not there in any other meaningful sense. I'm enclosed within the bubble of my own agendas, my own concerns, my own worries and anxieties.

Much of this book has been about making room in our life so we have some freedom from the various things that preoccupy us and prevent us from being fully present, whether they are concerns about money, worrying about work, dreaming about the next gadget to buy, or burying our head in our screens. It's true that modern life does throw up a lot of obstacles to paying full attention in our relationships. But it's also true that we're an easily distractible species, probably because we evolved to pay attention to a lot of variables in our landscape so we could find the food we needed, be good predators, and avoid being good prey. But it's *also* true that we have an exquisite capacity for focus and for paying real attention, for being fully present. And we can train and improve that capacity—with practice.

In any athletic endeavor, there are two main ways to improve. One is the general discipline of training your body so you have the strength, flexibility, coordination, and endurance your sport requires. The other is putting all those abilities into practice through the sport itself. To improve at a game, you have to play the game. It's similar with relationships. One of the best ways to really learn how to listen and be present in a relationship is to have some sort of general practice—spiritual practice—of sitting still, getting quiet, and paying attention. For me, mindfulness meditation and centering prayer have been really important daily spiritual practices that help make room for full attentiveness to the workings of my own soul and to the world around me. Those practices are very helpful at building up the general skills of attention, but they are, in the end, just practices. As hard as it may be to be mindful in the relatively controlled environment of a formal "sit" or period of prayer, it's another thing entirely to bring those skills off the meditation cushion and out into the wild world of relationships. I have to get out and play the game too. I have to make an effort to give Cyndi the gift of my full attention in the complicated zig-and-zag, push-and-pull of our daily relationship. The same is true for our relationships with the other-than-human world. We will never heal the wounds of this world and live rightly within the limits of this beautiful planet unless and until we really learn how to be as fully present to the soil and water and trees and other creatures as we hope and try to be in our human relationships. Mother Earth may not speak in a human voice, but we can learn to listen to her just as we can learn to listen to one another.

## VULNERABILITY

I wish that living fully into your relationships were simply a matter of learning to listen and bring full attention, which isn't easy but is definitely a skill you can learn. Just as necessary but much harder is to show up in your relationships as your most honest, most authentic self. At least for me, one of the biggest obstacles to that kind of presence is a mortal fear of taking off my personal armor and allowing myself to be vulnerable. As someone who is deeply invested in performing well, achieving goals, and being above reproach, I find it immensely difficult to let my defenses down and to be honest about my faults, fears, imperfections, griefs, and shadow—especially around those I want to impress or those who, like Cyndi, are close enough to really wound me if I do show a soft underbelly. That's the problem with true listening: you almost certainly are going to hear something you don't really want to hear. You are going to hear, as I have heard many, many times, that you're not nearly as nice or sensitive or clever or whatever as you thought you were, and it's going to be very hard to keep pretending that you are. The truth hurts.

But so does a lack of truth. The price of denying your vulnerability and staying armored up is very high—higher than you can possibly afford, if you want to have good relationships. The great irony is that trying to keep yourself safe and invulnerable is actually far more of a risk, not only for how you show up in relationships, but how you show up in the world generally. I know this because I've spent many years and much energy trying to play it safe in this regard—and I often still do. Playing it safe, though, is also playing small, and at least in my experience, playing small—that is, failing to show up authentically in meaningful relationships and in life—has ended up hurting me and my relationships far more than the ways I've been hurt by being vulnerable.

Marriage is an exquisite school for vulnerability, but so is rock climbing. I had been stuck at a certain climbing level for a while because I played it too safe. I would only make the next move when I was absolutely sure that my foothold or handhold would be secure and that I wouldn't fall. But as I tried harder routes, such "bomb-proof" holds simply weren't available. Ironically, when I couldn't be sure of the next move and I spent too much time pondering, often my grip on my current hold would give out, and I would fall anyway. When I finally started trusting that the rope would catch me even if I did fall, I was able to start making riskier, less certain, and more vulnerable moves, trying something even when I wasn't convinced that it would hold. Some of the time it didn't and I fell—and was safely caught by my belayer and the rope. Most of the time, however, the hold held. Sometimes you just have to trust and commit in spite of the risk.

I find it interesting that it's easier for me to screw up the courage to be vulnerable in the fear-for-your-life circumstances that rock climbing presents than it is in physically safe but emotionally fraught situations of human relationships and personal introspection. I know I'm not alone in this. In running an interfaith meditation center, I've encountered a lot of new meditators who begin a meditation practice and are very gung-ho about it. But a few weeks in, when the meditation honeymoon is over and all of their inner turmoil starts coming to the surface, they quit the practice, turning back to all the myriad activities that kept them safely distracted. They would rather be tossed to and fro by their overloaded life than be vulnerable in the face of things they'd rather not face. There, as the old saying goes, be dragons. But if Blaise Pascal was right that all of humanity's problems stem from an inability to sit quietly in a room alone, the dragons have to be faced for us to lead the fullest life possible. This is where simplicity can help, because if you choose a simpler path, you have fewer things to hide behind, such as an over-busy work schedule, the consumer treadmill, or your social media feed. Showing up authentically and vulnerably is never easy, but there are ways to make room for it by removing many of the ways that we dodge doing so.

## FORGIVENESS

When you do show up authentically and vulnerably in the world, you are going to get hurt. Period, full stop. There's no way around it, which is why so many of us are hesitant to put ourselves out there in the first place. I don't want to get hurt in relationships, so I often skate across the surface, hoping the thin ice holds. Because I don't want to be overwhelmed by grief at what we are doing to our hurting planet, I often don't connect deeply enough with the living world to really let in, as environmental activist Joanna Macy invites us, the immense gravity of that destruction.

Given the double-bind nature of vulnerability versus invulnerability, we're actually going to get hurt either way. To my mind, however, it's far better to suffer the wounds of showing up authentically than to suffer from an inability to connect.

But what do you do when you open yourself to your relationships and you get your heart broken? Because, of course, it's going to happen many, many times (and probably already has).

One of the things I so appreciate about contemplative spiritual practices like mindfulness and centering prayer is that at their core, they are about making room in your heart and mind to accept reality as it is. When you sit in silence, you inevitably end up being bombarded by the contents of your ruminating mind: past hurts and resentments, regrets, griefs—in other words, all of the ways in which reality has failed to live up to its end of the bargain. As I wrote above, it's that deluge of emotional flotsam and jetsam that often makes new meditators run for the hills. But the genius of these practices is the sage advice not to fight such feelings. Don't try to argue with reality, because reality will always win. What these practices recommend is simply noticing all this rumination, all these events that play on the movie screen of your mind, and accept them without judgment, without trying to change anything. This isn't to say that you end up being passive in the face of injustice or personal hurt. But any personal or societal change has to start by acknowledging the facts on the ground and working from there. What you resist, persists, according to psychologist Carl Jung. In other words, the more you fight demons inside and out, the more energy you feed them and, ironically, the stronger they get—and the more miserable and discontent you become. But if you can somehow make room in your psyche for the (often painful) truths that emerge in the clear sight of paying deep attention, somehow your noticing-and-accepting-without-judging, your very lack of agitated engagement begins to defang them.

Another name for this practice is forgiveness. The only way to keep showing up authentically and with simplicity amid the slings and arrows of relationships is to cultivate forgiveness for those who hurt you, forgiveness that your relationships, and just life in general, will disappoint and wound you. Entire volumes have been written on forgiveness, and I'm not qualified to dive into those deep waters, especially when it comes to genocide, rape, murder, abuse, and other egregious and seemingly unforgivable wrongs. What I'm getting at is a simple truth that we all know: life is not fair. Often, especially for us middle-classers in developed nations, we end up on the benefit side of the unfairness: What did we possibly do to deserve the happy accident of our birth and the kind of wealth and opportunity that's completely unimaginable to, say, a young girl in Afghanistan? But even we in the privileged classes can come up with a long list of grievances. Why did we get the alcoholic father, the corporate downsizing, the unfaithful spouse, the driver who crossed over the centerline into our lane, and all of the countless small and large hurts we've sustained from our parents, siblings, spouse, children, friends, coworkers, basically any human being with whom we've interacted?

Because life isn't fair. When we step out of the fairness/ unfairness paradigm, all of a sudden it becomes possible to accept other people and the world on their own terms, rather than according to our expectations. It becomes possible to turn the other cheek and forgive others—and even ourselves—for failures of various scopes and scales. It becomes possible to forgive life and the world for being the imperfect, unfair, paradoxical, contradictory, lovely mess that they are—that *we* are. It becomes possible to make room for all of this and to say a loving, grace-filled, unconditional yes to it all.

## GRATITUDE AND WONDER

Saying yes to your relationships with other human beings and with the entirety of creation may require the kind of true presence, vulnerability, and forgiveness that I've just described, but the true fuel of loving, authentic relationships is gratitude and wonder…or wonder and gratitude. As I've been thinking about this section, I've pondered which is the right order. That probably seems like a distinction without a difference, and of course both feed each other, but I think the order is important. Which comes first? Perhaps, especially when you've encountered an amazing sunset, or when you've received an absolutely gratuitous favor, or if you're still a child rather than a somewhat cynical adult, wonder will come first. Maybe you have the knack of walking through this wild world and simply being astonished by its magnificence, then falling to your knees and giving thanks. While I've had those kinds of experiences occasionally, that level of appreciation tends not to happen for me on a regular basis. Wonder, like creative inspiration, is not something that comes naturally to me. Plenty of days, my eyes are too tired to see anything but a tired world. Wonder is a God-given gift, not something you can manufacture any more than you can make yourself fall in love.

You can, however, build practices into your life that make it likelier for wonder to visit you—just as the regular practices of prayer and public worship can put you in a position where your heart is open enough to notice the burning bush, to hear the still small voice, to be touched by the wings of the angel, when such things occur. And the most fundamental of those practices is gratitude. Gratitude is the bedrock of simplicity, of healthy relationships, of love, of everything. Gratitude is what gives you the spaciousness to see that everything in your life is a gift, given to you by a Power beyond your imagining or your manipulation. And gratitude, I'm happy to say, is something you can get better at with practice.

There are plenty of ways to do this. I've kept a gratitude journal for years, in which, most mornings, I write down several things for which I'm grateful. They can be as mundane as the blessing of a decent night's sleep or as exalted as giving thanks for the miracle of my children. Cyndi and I try to express some sort of gratitude for each other throughout every day. Our family gathers for a short prayer time every evening, in which thanksgiving is the predominant theme. Many of these are for simple daily blessings, such as when our kids consistently give thanks for our long-haired cat and that he has stayed "fluffy."

You don't have to *feel* grateful—feelings are so fickle, anyway. You only need to give thanks on a daily basis for whatever is close at hand. And little by little, probably by the same divine grace that makes the garden grow, your capacity for giving thanks gets stronger. Your heart expands, with room in it to take in the blessed, beautiful brokenness of this world and all of the relationships that form it. From that increasingly fertile soil, wonder can grow.

There are many good reasons that you might try to make room in your life for the spaciousness of simplicity. As I've tried to show throughout these pages, a simpler life can be a source of abiding pleasure, satisfaction, meaning, and joy. It can be a path of ever-more authentic spirituality, opening our hearts so we can get in touch with the "really real" that so often gets crowded out and overpowered by the thrum of everyday distractions and obligations. Simplifying our affairs helps us to live in deeper solidarity with people who are poor, with future generations whose well-being depends on our actions, and with all the more-than-human members of our Earth community.

Fortunately, we're not without guides and counsel as we try to craft lives that are spacious, kind, and loving. A great cloud of witnesses from across the millennia and from across spiritual traditions have shown us what simplicity can look like when it's embodied in a particular human life and in a particular set of circumstances and relationships. I hope I've been able to offer you a few reflections that might help you as you walk this journey in your own unique way. I'm grateful to have been your walking companion for the time you've spent amid these pages, as we're both trying to figure these things out and live them the best we can.

## COSTING NOT LESS THAN EVERYTHING

In these pages, I've written about letting go of a lot of attachments: to money, to our work, to our stuff, to our digital lives, to our desire for self-sufficiency. To the extent we're able to loosen our grip in these ways, we have more room for authentic, loving relationships, which are the very nature of us, our world, and our Creator.

Letting go of our external attachments through simple living does help us to show up with our best selves. Finally, though, such lettings-go are prelude and path to the ultimate letting go, which costs not less than everything: our attachment to our own self. Of course, all of us will have to do this at the end of our days. But as Jesus, St. Francis, the Buddha, and plenty of other mystics and spiritual masters have taught and shown us, it's possible through practice to let go even in this life, to stop taking ourselves so seriously, to walk in the spacious freedom that comes from having nothing to prove, nothing to grasp at. In that condition of complete simplicity, which we may only experience in glimpses during this life, we find our truest belonging in and among all things and their Maker. And we know, as St. Julian did, that "all shall be well and all manner of thing shall be well."

## ONE: SIMPLE PLEASURES

What is your working definition of happiness? How is it the same as or different than fulfillment?

Describe a few times when you felt fully alive. What, if anything, did those moments have in common? What was present in them, and what was absent?

What are some of the most meaningful connections and relationships in your life, whether human or more-than-human? How do you nurture and sustain them?

## TWO: LETTING GO

Think about some of the significant losses you've experienced. How did you greet those losses? How did they change you? What lessons did they teach you?

What things in your life have you clung to too tightly? In what ways have those attachments gotten in the way of happiness, relationships, or other satisfactions?

Think of a time when you intentionally let something go that was important to you: a possession, a relationship, a job, an expectation. Why did you choose to let go? What happened? How did that letting go change you and your life?

Do you resonate with the idea that spiritual wisdom is more a process of letting go than a process of adding knowledge? Why or why not?

When have you been humiliated—not by another person, but by life itself? In such moments, were you able to open yourself to it? If so, how did that change you?

How do you understand the concept of "beginner's mind"? Can you think of any examples when you've held this attitude?

## THREE: FOR THE LOVE OF THE POOR

Have you experienced poverty personally? If so, how did it shape you? What is your attitude toward people who are poor?

In what ways are you—or might you find ways to be—in meaningful community with people who are poor?

Why do you think the Judeo-Christian Scriptures describe God as having a special love for the poor? Does God play favorites?

## FOUR: FOR THE LOVE OF THE EARTH

Think of an experience you've had of deep connection to the rest of the natural world. What made that experience so powerful? What kind of perspective did it give you on yourself and your place in the creation? What did it reveal to you about the Creator?

Do you experience yourself as being part and parcel with the rest of nature? Or do you think "nature" is something separate from humanity?

What regular practices do you do—or would you like to do—to connect in a meaningful way to the other-than-human world?

What does it mean to you to love the rest of the natural world?

## FIVE: MONEY

What does money represent for you? Security? Status? Power? Freedom? The means to generosity? Would you say you have a scarcity mentality or a sufficiency mentality, or something else? What sorts of experiences have formed your view of money?

In what ways would you claim to be wealthy? Why?

What sorts of meaningful activities do you do that are not reliant on money? Would their meaning be changed if money were more of a factor?

How do you understand the distinction between the Great Economy and the little economy?

In what ways does your dealing with money—your saving, sharing, and spending—line up or fail to line up with your values? What changes might you make so there is more alignment?

## SIX: WORK

In what ways has your work—whether paid or unpaid— helped you become your best self? In what ways, if any, has work revealed your sins and shortcomings?

What kinds of relationships have you been part of in connection to your work? In what ways have they been life-giving? In what ways have they been toxic?

Do you believe in the work you do? How, specifically, do you understand your work to contribute to a more flourishing world? If you can't answer that question in the affirmative, why do you continue this work?

What kinds of work do you do that you consider vital but

for which you aren't paid? Would you feel any differently about it if you were paid for it?

## SEVEN: PLAY

In what ways do you play as an adult? How is that life-giving for you?

What connections do you draw between play, humor, and the spiritual life? Do you understand prayer as a form of play? Why or why not? How easily can you picture a God who laughs and plays? If this is difficult for you to imagine, why do you think that is?

In our culture, play has often become commercialized and sports tend to be professionalized—witness the near-worship of sports figures and the high salaries they command. What is gained and lost in this?

## EIGHT: STUFF

Do you think the language of addiction is too strong to describe our relationship with stuff? Why or why not?

Almost everyone has a weakness when it comes to acquiring and hoarding stuff. What's yours? Where does it come from? What need does it fill in your life?

How do you understand the relationship between the material world and the spiritual world?

In what ways do your things hold memories and meaning for you? How do they serve your sense of solidarity with the poor and with the Earth?

If you have one, describe your process of inventorying and culling your things. When you do this, how does it feel?

### NINE: THE DIGITAL WORLD

How would you describe your relationship with digital technology? In what ways do you maintain healthy boundaries?

In what ways are you addicted to the digital world or is your relationship not healthy? What are the costs in your life of an unhealthy relationship with the digital world? What have you given up or lost?

What activities in your life lead to flow states? How do you carve out the time and space for those kinds of flow states to arise?

What might you need to change or let go of in order to have freedom and simplicity relative to the digital demands on your time and energy?

### TEN: RUGGED INTERDEPENDENCE

On page 111, the author writes: "Rugged independence is a myth, or else a very particular form of hell." Do you agree or disagree? Why?

To what degree do you think there is virtue in cultivating some degree of self-reliance? What does that "ruggedness" look like in your own life?

In what ways is your life intentionally, explicitly interdependent? How might it become more so? What social structures (extended family, neighborhood, workplace, worship community, etc.) support that interdependence?

In this chapter, the author plays with the ideas of complexity and simplicity, in many ways swapping them with each other. What forms of complexity do you think are worth nurturing in your life? What other forms of complexity do you have to let go of in order to do so?

## ELEVEN: FOOD

How would you describe your relationship with food? In what ways is it healthy? In what ways not?

What, if anything, do you do and say for your mealtime prayer? How do you—or how can you—make this into a regular opportunity to acknowledge the gift that food is from human and divine hands?

It's a strong statement to claim that we are "eating anger" when we eat the meat of creatures that have been raised inhumanely. Do you agree or disagree? If you agree, and if you still eat meat, how do you reconcile these things?

What are your rituals and practices in regard to meals at home? If you live with family, what do your common meals look like? If you live alone, how do you make mealtimes meaningful?

In what ways does your preparation of meals embody your values? Where are your growing edges in this area?

## TWELVE: RELATIONSHIPS

In what ways do you live your daily life out of a sense of individualism? On the flip side, what are some aspects of your life that are obviously and intentionally relational? How do you lean into relationships without losing yourself?

What daily spiritual practices—both formal and informal—do you use to cultivate a greater sense of presence and attentiveness?

How do you, to borrow a phrase from social science researcher and author Brené Brown, "rumble with vulnerability?" How have you been wounded when you've allowed yourself to be vulnerable? How have you suffered when you have refused to be vulnerable? What gifts has vulnerability offered you?

Think of a time in your life when you had to forgive someone for a serious hurt—even if they didn't seek forgiveness or weren't even alive to do so. How and why did you make the choice to forgive? How was it received, if at all? How did extending forgiveness change you?

In what ways do you cultivate gratitude in your life? How do you give thanks even for hard things? If you have had a gratitude discipline for any length of time, how has that affected you?

Brené Brown, *Daring Greatly: How the Courage to Be Vulnerable Transforms the Way We Live, Love, Parent, and Lead*. New York: Avery, 2015.

Charles Eisenstein, *The More Beautiful World Our Hearts Know Is Possible*. Berkeley, CA: North Atlantic Books, 2013.

Charles Eisenstein, *Climate Change: A New Story*. Berkeley, CA: North Atlantic Books, 2018.

Pope Francis, *Laudato Si': On Care for Our Common Home*. Huntington, IN: Our Sunday Visitor, 2015.

Hafiz, as rendered by Daniel Ladinsky, *I Heard God Laughing: Renderings of Hafiz*. New York: Penguin Books, 2006.

Marie Kondo, *The Life-Changing Magic of Tidying Up: The Japanese Art of Decluttering and Organizing*. Berkeley, CA: Ten Speed Press, 2014.

Cal Newport, *Deep Work: Rules for Focused Success in a Distracted World*. New York: Grand Central Publishing, 2016.

_____, *Digital Minimalism: Choosing a Focused Life in a Noisy World*. New York: Portfolio/Penguin, 2019.

Richard Rohr, *Falling Upward: A Spirituality for the Two Halves of Life*. San Francisco: Jossey-Bass, 2011.

E. F. Schumacher, *Small Is Beautiful: Economics as If People Mattered*. New York: Harper and Row, 1973.

Lynne Twist, *The Soul of Money: Reclaiming the Wealth of Our Inner Resources*. New York: W. W. Norton & Company, 2006.

Muhammad Yunus, *A World of Three Zeros: The New Economics of Zero Poverty, Zero Unemployment, and Zero Net Carbon Emissions*. New York: Hachette Book Group, 2017.

Franciscan Media is a nonprofit ministry of the Franciscan Friars of St. John the Baptist Province. Through the publication of spiritual books, *St. Anthony Messenger* magazine, and online media properties such as *Saint of the Day, Minute Meditations,* and *Faith & Family,* Franciscan Media seeks to share God's love in the spirit of St. Francis of Assisi. For more information, to support us, and to purchase our products, visit franciscanmedia.org.

*Live in love. Grow in faith.*

## About the Author

KYLE KRAMER is the Executive Director of the Passionist Earth & Spirit Center (www.earthandspiritcenter.org), which offers interfaith educational programming in meditation, ecology, and social compassion. Educated at Indiana University, the Universität Hamburg (Germany), and Emory University, he is the former director of graduate theology programs and spiritual formation for Saint Meinrad, a Benedictine monastery and Roman Catholic school of theology. Kyle and his family spent fifteen years as organic farmers and homesteaders in Spencer County, Indiana. Kyle serves as a Catholic Climate Ambassador for the USCCB-sponsored Catholic Climate Covenant and is the author of *A Time to Plant: Life Lessons in Work, Prayer, and Dirt* (Ave Maria Press, 2010). He is a former columnist and essayist for *America* magazine and a current columnist for Franciscan Media's *St. Anthony Messenger* magazine.